Tales of Old Warwickshire

Tales of Old Warwickshire

~

Betty Smith

With Illustrations by Don Osmond

COUNTRYSIDE BOOKS

NEWBURY, BERKSHIRE

First Published 1989
© Betty Smith 1989
Reprinted 1992, 1999, 2004

COUNTRYSIDE BOOKS
3 CATHERINE ROAD
NEWBURY, BERKSHIRE

ISBN 1 85306 052 6

Produced through MRM Associates Ltd., Reading
Typeset by Acorn Bookwork, Salisbury
Printed in England by J. W. Arrowsmith Ltd., Bristol

Bibliography

Warwickshire (Hickman 1979)
Warwickshire Villages (Lyndon F Cave 1976)
Rambles in Shakespeare's Country (J. H. Wade 1932)
Warwickshire (John Lisle 1936)
Haunted Warwickshire (Meg Elizabeth Atkins 1981)
Shakespeare Land (C. J. Ribton Turner 1893)
Bygone Warwickshire (Andrews 1893)
Historic Warwickshire (Burgess 1893)
Folklore of Warwickshire (Palmer 1976)
Princess Olive (Margaret Shepherd 1984)
Wroth Silver (R. T. Simpson 1927)
A Short History of Warwickshire & Birmingham (Bird 1977)
George Eliot (Kathleen Adams 1972)
Salford Hall (The Proprietors of Salford Hall 1968)
Tiddyoody Pie (F. W. Bennett 1930)
Highways & Byways in Shakespeare Country (Hutton 1914)
The Red Horse (Miller and Carrdus 1965)
Stratford on Avon Herald
Leamington Spa Courier
Evesham Journal
Focus Magazine (Stratford)
Many church and village 'booklets', plus many miscellanous
    items in the care of local archivists.

Contents

WARWICKSHIRE – The map overleaf is by John Speede and shows the county as it was in the early seventeenth century.

The
Red Horse
of Tysoe

NOT many people know that Warwickshire once had a great horse figure cut into its hillsides. Most people know of the various famous white horses, but there have been few red ones, and sad to relate our own has now disappeared.

He has, however, given his name to the Vale of the Red Horse, an especially beautiful and fertile tract of land lying snugly tucked below the Edgehill escarpment on the borders of Warwickshire and Oxfordshire.

The great red horse was lost sometime in the year 1800, and is now almost certainly lost to us forever, since the slopes across which he galloped have all been afforested.

The Warwickshire Red Horse was an acre in extent, and its true location was on the hillside above the village of Tysoe, between Spring Hill and Sun Rising Hill. It was red only because the soil on the hillside is naturally red in colour, and a particularly bright red when the sun shines upon it.

It is believed that the village of Tysoe takes its name from the Saxon Horse God 'Tui' and that it must have once been an early settlement of the horse people, who worshipped the great god Tui, and in his honour cut his image in the hillside beneath which they lived.

The great galloping figure was 'scoured', that is to say cleared of encroaching vegetation, as part of a spring rite each year. It is significant that the two hillsides are called Spring Hill and Sun Rising Hill. It is also significant perhaps that the location of the great horse is on a ley line pointing to where the sun rises at the vernal equinox.

After Christianity came to our shores, the scouring of the great red horse still continued, only now it was done on Palm Sunday. The Church, unable to prevent the continuation of pagan rites and beliefs, tended to acquire them unto itself. Thus with our red horse. In pre-Christian days when it was scoured, the villagers, worshippers, sacrificed to the god Tui hoping to ensure good crops, plentiful food and the survival of their tribe. As time went on, it became the Palm Sunday feast and a certain amount of jollification attended it.

The earliest written reference to the Red Horse of Tysoe was in 1606 by the cartographer John Speed, who wrote '. . . corn as the chiefest commodity whereof the Red Horse Vale yieldeth most abundantly. . . .'

The following year, that intrepid traveller, Camden in his *Britannia* (1607) wrote a trifle patronisingly of '. . . the shape of a horse cut in a red hill by countery people hard by Pillerton. . . .'

Camden was at this time travelling down the old Roman road, the Fosseway just north of Pillerton, so that the figure on the hillside must have been visible to him from a distance of some four miles.

Sir William Dugdale, the notable Warwickshire historian, who was so active during the Civil War, saw the red horse at the Battle of Edgehill in 1642, and later wrote in his *Antiquities of Warwickshire*:

'. . . there is cut upon the side of Edgehill in the proportion of a horse in a very large forme which by reason of the ruddy colour of the earth is called the Red Horse and giveth denomination to the fruitful and pleasant country hereabouts. . . .'

In 1767, Richard Jago, one-time vicar of Snitterfield, wrote an epic poem about Edgehill, He was not in the forefront of our ranks of poets, and the work is long and boring; but he saw the horse figure as some kind of sign of not only Saxon rule, but Celtic slavery:

> 'And Tysoe's wondrous theme, the martial Horse
> Carved on the yielding turf
> Armorial sign of Hengist, Saxon Chief
> Studious to preserve
> The Fav'rite form, the treach'rous conquerors
> Their vassal tribes compel with festive rites
> Its fading figure yearly to renew
> And to the neighbouring Vale impart its name.'

Hengist and Horsa were two brothers who led the first band of Teutonic invaders to this country. True, both names mean 'horse', but whether they ever got any further north than Kent is very uncertain.

There was also an old legend, fostered by a couple of Oxfordshire clergymen, that the figure had been cut into the hillside by the Earl of Warwick when he was returning from the bloodiest battle of the Wars of the Roses, Towton Field, on Palm Sunday 1461. It is said that the Earl's horse fell, on this very hillside, as his master was heading back home to Warwick, and thus did the Earl commemorate the work of his valiant old war horse.

This could not, however, be true, since traces of the old horse have shown that it is far older than this.

In the year 1800, one Simon Nicholls purchased the pub called the Sun Rising Inn, which stands on top of the hill which bears its name. Simon Nicholls was a successful and hard-working landlord, and from far and wide his customers came, to taste his excellent ale and partake of his liberal table. When the horse was scoured on Palm Sundays, Simon Nicholls did a roaring trade in cakes and ale, and in fact, it developed into a bit of a feast day.

Strange to relate, therefore, that Simon Nicholls it was who ploughed up the great red horse. He got tired of what he thought of as a 'peasant' task, scouring and keeping it clean. He fondly imagined that everyone would turn up at the inn just because it was Palm Sunday, red horse or no red horse. So in the time of the spring ploughing, Simons Nicholls ploughed up the great horse figure cut into the hillside more than a thousand years before. There were no preservation orders then. Simon Nicholls was a philistine, and no one could stop him. It was his land.

He should have known better; without the great red galloping horse what reason was there for the Palm Sunday cakes and ale? It might as well just be an ordinary Palm Sunday down in the village, around the church. So the people did not come, and Nicholls' trade declined.

In desperation, he cut another horse figure, smaller, and closer to his own inn, but it was no good. People knew what he was about, and they were not fooled. Eventually, the smaller horse figure too disappeared into the hillside from where it emerged.

Much careful and studied research has been carried out in recent years to establish the exact location of the great Red Horse of Tysoe. There was some urgency, since the Forestry Commission planted the hillsides, and it was thought the spreading roots of the trees would obliterate anything that might have survived. Aerial photographs were taken, and soil and vegetation tests made.

Eventually, it was discovered that no less than five horse figures had once graced the hillside, with the original one, the Saxon one, taking pride of place and being the largest and oldest.

However, the great horse, once referred to by the vicar of Banbury as the 'Nag of Renown' is gone; lost forever, just because Simon Nicholls was lazy. But at least the hillside across which the great Red Horse loped, head held high, is still verdant and beautiful, and 'yieldeth abundantly'.

14

The Siege of Caldecote Hall

THE small village of Caldecote lies on the boundary of the county, and on the east bank of the river Anker there once stood an old manor house, Caldecote Hall, home of the Purefoy family. It was here in August 1642 that Dame Joan Purefoy, a handful of maids and a handful of men, held the Hall against the onslaught of Prince Rupert and 18 troops of horse, and so saved the life of her husband.

Colonel William Purefoy was an ardent and vigorous Puritan. He represented the Borough of Warwick in the Long Parliament, was engaged in the defence of Warwick Castle against the King, and had been boldly outspoken in Parliament against the taxes levied by the King upon his subjects. He had become a marked man.

In August 1642 the King was at Coventry, where the citizens had not been at all pleased to see him, and where he received no welcome. Prince Rupert was riding into Warwickshire, and the garrison at Warwick Castle under command of Sir Edward Peto was expecting to be besieged at almost any day. The Parliamentarian Lord Brooke was riding around the Midlands trying to recruit more men to their cause to help in the defence of the castle, and Colonel William Purefoy was on the same errand when, on 28th August 1642, he chose to visit his wife at Caldecote Hall.

15

The 28th was the Sabbath, and Colonel William was walking in the gardens of the Hall, talking to the vicar of Caldecote, Richard Vines. Vines was a fanatical Puritan, and was attempting to persuade Colonel William to have the bells removed from the church as 'tongues of the devil'.

A young servant lad climbed to the top of the tower, the better to see the view on this wonderful sunny morning. What he did see in the distance was the sun shining on the helmets of Prince Rupert's soldiers as they neared the Hall. He rushed down from the tower to warn his master. Richard Vines immediately reproved him for being so sinful as to climb the tower on the Sabbath, but the Colonel was more generous and thanked the lad.

There was a hurried conference. What was to be done? The Colonel had no doubt that the Prince and his men had come to take him prisoner, and the Prince was a man to be reckoned with!

George Abbott, Purefoy's son-in-law, took command of the situation. He too was a Puritan, and was determined to save the Colonel, whom he held in great affection.

A hiding place had long been prepared for just such a contingency in the hop garden, where a hole had been dug out, and the whole thing well disguised with old hop poles and growing vegetation. The Colonel was taken there and hidden, with instructions on pain of his life, and the lives of all of them, not to emerge until someone came to collect him.

George Abbott and his mother-in-law, Dame Joan, called all their people together, and explained what was likely to happen. In great haste instructions were given, and retainers ran hither and thither, gathering up great feather beds to block up the windows, and barricading the doors.

The cook was told to build up a huge fire and to start melting down all the pewter spoons and plates to make bullets. They had a few guns in the house, and a little powder, but scarcely any shot. The men and the women servants were all given rapid instructions on how to load and fire a gun.

They had scarce completed these primitive preparations,

when the sound of horses' hooves was heard on the road leading up to the Hall. A trumpet sounded, and four Officers rode up to the great door. 'What do you want disturbing Godly people on the Sabbath,' cried Dame Joan, as she opened the wicket to them.

The Officers demanded entrance in the name of Prince Rupert, to search for the 'rebel Colonel Purefoy'. 'Begone', cried Dame Joan grandly, and made to close the wicket. However, the Officers rushed forward, and said they would have admittance. Whereupon, Dame Joan, crying 'May God forgive me', raised the gun at her side, aimed and pulled the trigger. One of the Officers fell from his horse, and the other three beat a hasty retreat.

George Abbott, anticipating that the Royalist would next try to break in through the courtyard, stationed himself there with four men. He was proved right. The gates burst open and the Royalist troopers charged in with battering poles, ready to break down the great door and gain admittance to the Hall.

George Abbott and his four loyal servants fired, were handed reloaded guns by the women, and fired again. And again. Troopers fell before the concentrated onslaught of this handful of men, and eventually cleared out of the courtyard, dragging their wounded with them.

The Royalists then gathered straw and set it against the house, seeking to divert attention from the courtyard by firing the straw. But again they were thwarted by brave George Abbott and the courageous four.

The tiny garrison inside the Hall held out for two more onslaughts, but they knew they would have to give in. They had run out of powder, and the bullets hurriedly contrived from the family pewter were all used up. The Royalist troopers then set fire to the buildings on the edge of the courtyard and the flames roared upwards, spreading rapidly in the direction of the Hall itself. 'We can fight no more', declared George Abbott, and Dame Joan agreed that maybe it was for the best and perhaps lives would be spared if they conceded.

Just then the Cavaliers gathered again, and headed by

Prince Rupert himself, prepared to make a further charge against the Hall. As they neared, Dame Joan swung wide the great door, and rushing forward, flung herself at the feet of the Prince, beseeching him not to harm a 'handful of women'.

The Prince and his Officers could scarce believe they had been held off for so long by Dame Joan, George Abbott, four men and a few serving maids. Magnanimously, he commended them for the brave defence of their home.

He said he must have the Colonel and ordered the Hall to be thoroughly searched from top to bottom, but he decided 'the bird had flown'. His soldiers wanted to sack and destroy the house, as they usually did, to prevent it being regarrisoned and so used against them at a later date, but the Prince would not allow this. He said it had been bravely defended and bravery and courage should be honoured. He spared both the Hall and the lives of all within it.

He went even further, and tried to persuade George Abbott to go along with him, and to take command of a troop of Royalist horse. Politely George Abbott declined, saying he was of another persuasion, and his conscience would not allow him to fight on the Royalist side. This too the Prince accepted, and said that the consciences of brave men commanded respect. He gathered his troopers, their dead and wounded, and rode off towards Coventry, leaving behind a handful of exhausted men and women.

The fire was gaining hold, and when the troopers had left, villagers from nearby rushed to help put out the fire. When darkness fell, the Colonel was collected from the hiding place where he had remained safely hidden and, mounting a borrowed horse, he rode off towards Northampton and Lord Brooke.

Colonel Purefoy survived the Civil War, and was one of the signatories to the death warrant of King Charles I. The battle-scarred front door of the old Hall was, sometime later, put inside the church to remind all who saw it of the valiant defence of Caldecote Hall.

The Tapestry Weavers of Barcheston

THE tiny village of Barcheston lies just to the south of the market town of Shipston-on-Stour, and visitors, of whom there are but few, are astonished when they learn that in this depopulated village where there remains no more than a church and a handful of dwellings, a tapestry weaving industry began in Tudor times that lasted more than a century.

Inside the church, high on the wall, is all that remains of the enterprise, a small plaque to Richard and Francis Hyckes:

'Master weavers who in succession had charge of tapestry looms set up at Barcheston by William Sheldon of Beoley'.

The Sheldon family is a very old and honourable one, and it is thought they originally had connections with Sheldon, near Birmingham. Like most such families their roots were embedded firmly in the soil; they came of yeoman stock, but they deliberately sought to improve their status by judicious and prudent marriages, and in this they succeeded.

William Sheldon of Beoley, the man named on the Hyckes plaque, took as his wife the daughter of William and Anne Willington of Barcheston, and upon the death of his father-in-law, he acquired the adjoining manors of Barcheston and Willington. He already owned Weston Park, and he it was that was granted licence to 'empark' the land. The Willingtons had six daughters, all of whom married exceedingly well, so that William Sheldon was connected by marriage to all the best Midland families.

William Sheldon seems to have been a vigorous and energetic man, and of the 'doing' kind. At some stage in the years 1554/5 he sent his son, Ralph, accompanied by Richard Hyckes, a native of Barcheston, to travel on the Continent, partly to widen the young man's education, but also with firm instructions to learn all he could about the art of Flemish tapestry weaving.

Anthony-a-Wood, a noted diarist and friend of a later generation of Sheldons, wrote that Hyckes was 'bound 'prentice to a Dutch arras weaver. . . .' which may or may not have been the truth. Certainly one would suppose that it was the most acceptable and straightforward way to learn such skills.

When Ralph Sheldon and Richard Hyckes returned, they reported on their travels to William Sheldon, who immediately gave Richard Hyckes the job of discovering, acquiring and buying suitable looms and setting them up in the manor house at Barcheston. Hyckes brought back with him a man always referred to as 'Peter the Dutchman', who might also have been involved in tapestry weaving. Certainly his name must have been too difficult for rural Warwickshire tongues, since throughout the records he is named simply just that.

Hyckes then set about gathering together a small group of villagers at Barcheston, and proceeded to teach them all he had learned about the art and skill of tapestry weaving.

A man called William Dowler was appointed Hyckes's assistant, and is the only one of them referred to in Sheldon's will where he is called '. . . the only anter and beyginner of this arte within this Realme . . .'

Sheldon gave him free lodging at the manor house '. . . chiefly in respect of the maytenance of making tapestries, arras, moccadoes, carolles, plunketts, Grogaynes, sayes and sarges. . . .' He described the industry as '. . . a trade greatley beneficial to this commonwealth to trade youthe in and a meane to secure great summes of money within this Realme . . . '

So William Sheldon was in it for investment, and because he sought to bring a trade to a small rural area where there was otherwise little work. There were Flemish weavers at work in London at this period, but it is believed that the patriotic Sheldon wished to prove that Englishmen could do the work with equal skill, if properly taught. No foreign names appear in the old records of Barcheston during this period, other than Peter the Dutchman, and it is believed that all the tapestries which eventually came off the Barcheston looms were woven by English, and indeed Warwickshire, hands.

It soon became clear that Sheldon's confidence had not been misplaced. Richard Hyckes rapidly acquired an enviable reputation in the art of tapestry weaving, and by 1570 when Sheldon died, many fine works had already been completed. Sheldon left explicit instructions to his heir, Ralph, to continue the industry and instructed him to ensure that certain of the tapestries would hang in the family's Worcestershire seat at Beoley 'from heire to heire . . .'

Francis Hyckes, son of Richard, was a student at St Mary Hall, Oxford, but it is clear that whilst ensuring that his son received the more formal education due to a young man of his status, his father also passed on to him his skill in weaving.

Richard Hyckes continued in charge of the Barcheston looms until his death in 1621 at the ripe old age of 97. Then Francis, who had long been working with his father, took over the operation.

The fame of the Warwickshire weavers had obviously spread as far as the Royal household, for in 1584/5 Richard and Francis Hyckes were summoned to the court of Queen Elizabeth I and called upon to repair tapestries in the Tower, Westminster, Hampton Court, Richmond, Windsor and other Royal residences, with material which was specially woven at Barcheston.

The most notable of the works produced at Barcheston are the tapestry maps. These are fairly large, approximately 13 ft by 17 ft, and have decorative borders reminiscent of Renaissance art. Some have figures from classical mythology, and some of them have 'Ric Hyckes' woven into one corner.

Eventually maps were made of almost all the Midland counties: Warwickshire, Gloucestershire, Herefordshire, Worcestershire, Derbyshire, and Staffordshire.

The map of Warwickshire is in the keeping of the Warwickshire County Museum, where it graces one large wall. No longer quite so colourful as when it first came from the Barcheston looms, but greatly pleasing, it was presented to the county as a gift from the Courtauld Institute some years ago.

The *Four Seasons* tapestry at Hatfield House is thought to be a Sheldon woven at Barcheston; the Ashmolean Museum at Oxford has one or two examples of the work. Further pieces are at Chastleton House in Oxfordshire, and Sudeley Castle, near Winchcombe, Gloucestershire.

The *Coronation of the Blessed Virgin* hangs at Compton Wynyates, the home of the Marquess of Northampton, and *Judah giving his Staff and Bracelets to Tamar* (c.1595) hangs in Aston Hall, Birmingham. There are also some examples on permanent view in the Victoria and Albert Museum in London.

Another Ralph Sheldon, great-great-grandson of William, born 1623, is perhaps the best known of this family, and is always referred to as the 'Great Sheldon'.

The Sheldons suffered greatly during the Civil War, and the Commonwealth, because of their Catholic faith and their adherence to the King. Ralph (the Great) only came into his inheritance with the Restoration in 1660. The Great Sheldon married Henrietta Maria, daughter of Lord Rocksavage, but the marriage was childless, and when the lady sadly died of the plague, Ralph Sheldon did not seek another wife.

His funeral, arranged by Anthony-a-Wood, was impressive, with the body lying in state for a whole week, and then the long funeral procession on foot the many miles between Weston Park and Beoley, Worcestershire.

Whilst the body was taken to Beoley, by his own request,

the Great Sheldon's heart and viscera were buried in the church at Long Compton, the parish church of his beloved Weston Park, where he ended his days.

The church at Long Compton was restored in 1861, when three small red velvet caskets were discovered beneath the altar slabs, each containing the heart and viscera of one of the Sheldons of Weston Park. They were reverently replaced and remain there still, undisturbed.

With the end of the Great Sheldon, came an end to the tapestry weaving. The Civil War had wrought havoc in the countryside; there had been much movement and much destruction. When Ralph Sheldon again came into his own, it was too late. With his death the estate passed out of the direct line, and the Sheldon who inherited came from outside the county and did not seek to continue the industry. In all it had lasted for a hundred years, but the wonderful works supervised by both Richard and Francis Hyckes have outlasted all of them.

Perhaps the Great Sheldon knew, for he wrote his own epitaph thus:

'Once Ralph Sheldon. Now ashes, dust, nothing.'

Witchcraft on Meon

MEON Hill rises green and softly cushioned above the village of Lower Quinton, on the Warwickshire fringes of the Cotswolds. It is a place of changing scene and shifting mood, whose smiling face in the mellow sunlight of a summer day gives little indication of the mysteries the centuries have heaped upon its head.

Meon Hill is a place of faerie, of legend and superstition, and we are told that it is on Meon Hill that witches still hold their sabbats.

Meon Hill was the scene of this country's most famous witchcraft murder, which to this day remains unsolved.

It was on the feast of St Valentine, 14th February 1945, that the body of a 74 year old hedge cutter, Charles Walton, was discovered beneath an oak tree on Meon. He had been brutally murdered with a billhook which was still embedded in the wounds upon his body. But horror increased when it was discovered that Walton's throat had been cut in the form of a cross, and his body pinned firmly to the ground with a hayfork, the prongs passing through the skin of the neck, and the handle thrust into the hedge to hold it steady. In that way the blood from the murder wounds ran down the iron of the hay fork and into the ground.

Police were completely baffled by this dreadful and apparently motiveless murder. For who could want to kill Charles Walton?

He was, to all intents and purposes, a harmless old man. A native of Lower Quinton, he was a 'loner' and sought solitude, but so do most countrymen, and Charles Walton was a true countryman, with a love of nature and a passion for the soil that town dwellers can never fully comprehend.

Villagers thought of him as 'irritable' and a bit 'testy' and they considered it strange that he did not drink in the local pubs as did other farm workers. Instead, Walton preferred to buy draught cider and drink it at home. His wife had died many years before, and his niece Edith kept house for him.

Walton earned an average rate of 1s 6d an hour when he worked, and because he was seen to spend so little, rumour grew that his wife had left him some money, and that he was a 'warm' man with a 'bit of silver' tucked away.

The police set about their task with accustomed expertise, convinced the murderer must be a local man, and in a village of no more than 400 souls, not too difficult to track down. Superintendent Alec Spooner of Warwickshire CID took charge, and two days later Detective-Superintendent Robert Fabian of Scotland Yard arrived on the scene.

Fabian of the Yard, a man of vast experience in murder enquiries, could make no headway. He reckoned without the Warwickshire villagers, who flatly refused to talk. They remained passively unco-operative, insisting only that 'We all know us, and it isn't one of us or we'd know . . .'

Then Fabian came up against the famed 'black dog' of Quinton, a creature that features largely in stories of witchcraft and the occult in these parts. Fabian, who did not believe in any such nonsense, was soon to learn that to the people of Meon it was all very real.

He was on Meon, searching for any clues that might possibly have been missed, when a large black dog ran past him. A couple of minutes later a young lad who worked on a local farm appeared, and Fabian asked him if he was looking for his dog!

'What dog?' asked the youth.

'A big black dog that just came past me here', said Fabian in a friendly way.

To his astonishment, the youth immediately went deathly pale and ran off without answering. The detective thought little of what appeared to be a trivial incident, but brought the subject up that evening in the local pub.

He was then told that no one talked of the black dog of Quinton, and the last one that admitted seeing it was the dead and murdered Charles Walton, years before when he was a much younger plough lad. 'He saw the black dog', they told him, 'and two days later his sister died suddenly.'

Fabian was about to smile and turn the whole thing into a bar-room joke, but realised that a silence had fallen on the room, and one by one the regulars left the pub.

He was to hear more of the black dog, for shortly after this another killing took place on Meon and the body of a large black dog was found hanged by its own collar from the branch of the tree above the spot where Charles Walton's body was found.

The day after this, a police car negotiating the narrow lanes around Lower Quinton ran over a large black dog and killed it. Then a heifer belonging to a local farmer was found dead in a ditch, and the villagers whispered about witchcraft and black magic, and went around stony-faced.

Fabian maintained he did not believe in this 'witchcraft nonsense' but the people of Lower Quinton did, and to them he was an offcomer, the stranger in their midst. Fabian found cottage doors closed to him, and Lower Quinton established a wall of silence.

The date of the murder could be important if this was indeed a witchcraft killing. In 1945, the feast of St Valentine and Ash Wednesday fell upon the same day. At this time of year, it was the custom in ancient times for adherents of the old faith (before Christianity came to these shores) to offer sacrifices of newly-spilled blood to the soil to ensure good crops. Fabian himself said Walton's injuries were so hideous it looked like the kind of killing Druids might have done in a ghastly ceremony at full moon.

The style of the killing followed almost exactly the pattern of a witchcraft murder some 70 years earlier. Then an alleged witch from nearby Long Compton was killed by a farm labourer who maintained she had brought ill luck to him and his family by casting spells upon them.

Police persevered with their intensive investigations, but despite taking more than 4,000 separate statements, tracing tinkers and gypsies believed to have been in the area at the time, and questioning prisoners of war at a nearby camp, they got nowhere.

Aerial photographs were taken by an Avro Anson plane from Leamington and Royal Engineers from the nearby army camp combed the hedges and ditches with mine detectors, seeking Charles Walton's missing old tin watch.

They discovered one suspect, an Italian POW, whose mates had found him trying to get bloodstains off his clothing. He was also seen crouching in a ditch near the murder spot. Police questioned the man who said he had been out after rabbits. They sent his clothing for forensic tests, and found – rabbit's blood. Then he took them to the spot where he had set snares, and they were convinced and let him go!

In total some 29 samples of hair and clothing were forensically tested, and all to no avail. Charles Walton was buried in the little churchyard at Lower Quinton, and his murderer walked freely.

Alec Spooner never gave up though. Every 14th February for the next 15 years until his retirement, he turned up at Lower Quinton and wandered around the murder spot, standing beneath a nearby willow tree that came to be known locally as Spooner's willow.

Villagers adopted the theory that he was doing this to wear the murderer down, to make him take some action, panic him into making a mistake that would reveal his identity. The inhabitants of Lower Quinton had buried Charles Walton, and they did not want to be reminded of the facts surrounding his death. But Spooner didn't want the murderer to forget either. No case is closed until it is solved, and the file remains open on the Meon Hill murder.

The
Murder of
Sir Thomas Overbury

O N 15th September in the year 1613, Warwickshire's Sir
Thomas Overbury died in the Tower of London at the
age of 32. He was, it is said, reduced to skin and bone, and was
incarcerated in a dark, dank, unwholesome cell from which he
never even saw the light of day. Yet his death might have
passed unnoticed had it not been for a disgruntled errand boy.

Sir Thomas was the second son of Sir Nicholas Overbury,
and his elder brother having died, he was his father's heir. His
mother was the daughter of Giles Palmer of Compton Scorpion, near Ilmington, in Warwickshire. It was here at Compton Scorpion that Sir Thomas was born in 1581. He was
educated according to his station in life, matriculating at the
age of 14 at Queen's College, Oxford, and graduating as a
BA some three years later.

Sometime around 1601 Thomas and a travelling companion went on holiday to Edinburgh, where Overbury was
introduced to a young man of about his own age. The friendship which sprang up between them was eventually to lead to
the downfall and death of Sir Thomas, for this young man was
Robert Carr, at that time page to the Earl of Dunbar.

Robert Carr was a personable young man with ambitions,
and it didn't take him very long to realise which side his bread
was buttered. He managed to capture the attention of King

James VI, and in 1603 was invited to accompany the King, now also James I of England, to London. This he was only too ready to do, and he began to ingratiate himself with the King, so that he received many gifts and favours. His prosperity increased, and what more natural then that he should send for his friend Overbury and secure for him a favoured position at Court.

Robert Carr was both clever and crafty, but he was no scholar, and it was to Overbury he turned for help in this direction.

In 1610 Carr was created Viscount Rochester and Overbury must then have thought preferment would also be offered to him, for at the Court of King James only by favour and patronage could anyone aspire to office and prosperity. Even Francis Bacon is said to have attempted to cultivate Overbury, and through him Rochester, for favours.

Overbury's star seemed in the ascendant, but Rochester proceeded to fall in love with a lady whose reputation was far from unsullied – Frances Howard, Countess of Essex. Overbury, at his friend's behest, wrote many letters, and composed poetry in honour of this lady, Rochester being unable to attain such scholarly heights. Romantic intrigue was the order of the day at Court and Overbury had no qualms about writing letters supposedly from Rochester, nor writing poetry which the Countess fancied came from the pen of Rochester.

Overbury was brought up short when the Countess divorced her husband and publicly announced her intention of marrying Rochester. Overbury thought the lady would serve very well as a romantic mistress, but that marriage between them would mean nothing but disaster. He tried to dissuade his friend, but to no avail. It is doubtful if Rochester intended marriage at first, but he was ultimately forced into it by the lady's constant declarations. He fell completely beneath her spell; she was very dominating, and he was weak. It was even later suggested that Frances Howard had used witchcraft to gain a hold over Rochester.

The strong and vociferous protests made by Overbury

against the marriage caused a breach in the long-standing friendship between the two men and Rochester, anxious to be rid of Overbury, arranged for him to be offered a position abroad. But Overbury declined, and this brought him into disfavour with the King.

Overbury made a nuisance of himself to his friend, and refused to take any part in their much publicised marriage plans. So much of a nuisance did he become that Rochester and the lady had him flung into the Tower on 26th April 1613.

Rochester thought of it as a temporary convenience, but the Lady Frances took and entirely different view. She had no intention of ever allowing Overbury to come between her and her desires again, and she had already laid her plans for his murder.

She contrived the dismissal of the Lieutenant of the Tower, a man of integrity, and she replaced him with one of her own minions. She provided a man called Richard Weston to attend upon Overbury and serve his food. So began the slow and insidious poisoning. A deadly mixture of mercury and white arsenic was to be mixed in with the prisoner's food.

Sir Thomas had not been in very good health when he went into the Tower, but now he wrote that his bodily torments were beyond belief, although at no time does he seem to have suspected the cause. Medical knowledge was somewhat scanty, and the two medical men called into examine Overbury put his condition down to his incarceration and nothing else.

Eventually the Lady Frances thought it had gone on long enough, and the last fatal dose was administered. Sir Thomas died alone and in agony. His death was ascribed to 'natural' causes, and within a few short hours of drawing his last breath, he was buried within the perimeter of the Tower.

In December Rochester and the Lady Frances were married, and there the whole affair might have rested, but for the errand boy. He ran messages for the apothecary who had supplied the drugs, and fancied he had a grievance. He talked in the alehouses and he talked among his cronies, until at last it came to the ears of authority, and investigations began.

Sir Thomas had been imprisoned in the Tower for almost six months, without charge or trial, and eventually the full evil of the Lady Frances and her minions was discovered. Rochester and his lady were brought to trial and imprisoned, but the King, to whom Rochester was still a favourite, subsequently released and pardoned them both. The rest of the plotters were executed.

Sir Nicholas Overbury outlived his murdered son by 30 years, and upon his death his estate was inherited by another Sir Thomas, nephew and namesake of the unfortunate victim. This Sir Thomas, a country gentleman in every sense of the word, was knighted in 1660, died in 1684, and is buried at Lower Quinton, not far from Stratford-on-Avon in Warwickshire.

Warwickshire's 'Other' Poet

So synonymous has Warwickshire become with the legend of the great William Shakespeare that many people do not realise that we did have other writers and poets, among whom Michael Drayton looms large. He was just about a year older than Shakespeare, and was writing at about the same time.

Michael Drayton was born in March 1563 in the village of Hartshill in the north of the county, and he was of yeoman stock. In his various letters he refers to himself as being 'well connected', although Aubrey in his *Brief Lives* calls him a 'butcher's sonne'. But he also referred in similar vein to William Shakespeare. Drayton family wills prove them to have been a family of some substance, and they were certainly a prolific clan.

At an early age, Drayton was placed in the household of Sir Henry Goodere of Polesworth, initially as a page, and during this period he attended the Abbey Gatehouse School there, rapidly acquiring a love of learning and of scholarship. Raphael Holinshed, the famous chronicler and noted scholar lived close to Polesworth at this time, and his influence is thought to have contributed largely to Drayton's scholarship. Certainly they knew each other, met and talked.

The Goodere family was an exceedingly rich and powerful one. In 1571 Henry Goodere was returned MP for Coventry, and in this same year he was also committed to the Tower for unlawful dealings with Mary, Queen of Scots. However, his incarceration was not a lengthy one, and he was back home again in time for the birth of his daughter, Anne, who was to be Michael Drayton's lifelong love and the inspiration, so it is thought, for much of his poetry.

Drayton, eight years older than Anne, must have watched the little girl growing from babyhood, taking her first steps, and it is highly probable that he helped in her first lessons. When he first fell in love with her, he does not say; nor is there any evidence at all that Anne returned his love, or thought of him as anything other than a dear friend and companion of her childhood.

In 1594 when Anne was almost 23, Drayton published a series of sonnets called *Idea's Mirrour* and there is little doubt that Anne herself was the 'Idea' of whom he wrote. The sonnets, written from a pure heart, express the love of a young man for that which he sees as unattainable.

> 'Virtue's Idea in virginitie
> By inspiration came conceived with thought
> The time is come when delivered she must be
> Where first my love into the world was brought.'

And it was Idea's eyes (Anne's) which '. . . . taught mee the alphabet of love. . . .'

Poetry in Drayton's time held an honourable place, not only in literature, but in polite society. Many ladies and gentlemen 'dabbled' in verse, and much verse was written to be handed around and read aloud rather than to be published. Poets lived in the houses of great families, and held privileged offices as tutors, secretaries, companions, and in return they dedicated their latest batch of verses to their patron, or to his family. Without patronage it is likely they would have starved, at least some of the time!

In the following year, Drayton wrote *The Shepherd's Garland* with several parts and a chorus, casting himself in the role of 'Rowland of the Rock'. This refers to the village of his birth,

Hartshill, and the rock quarrying there. Rowland's mistress in the piece was again 'Idea'.

Alas for poor Michael Drayton, in 1595 Anne Goodere married Henry Rainsford, a young squire five years her junior. The couple made their home in the old black and white timbered manor house at Clifford Chambers, just two miles from Stratford-on-Avon.

It was here that Drayton would stay each summer, in the same house as his beloved 'Idea', and in 1612, in perhaps the work for which he is best remembered, *Polyolbion*, he refers to the nearby Vale of Evesham and the Cotswolds:

> 'Deere Cliffords seat, the place of health and sport
> Which many a time hath been the Muses Quiet Port.'

It was in the old house at Clifford that Drayton talked with Ben Jonson, and with Shakespeare, both of whom were frequent visitors. It was here too that Michael Drayton was attended by Dr John Hall, physician, and son-in-law to Shakespeare. The doctor wrote in his case book: 'Mr Drayton, an excellent poet, labouring of a tertian was cured by an emetic infusion of syrup of violets'. It has always seemed appropriate that syrup of violets should have been the right medicine for a poet!

Anne's husband was knighted with others at the Coronation of James I. They were married for 27 years, and had three sons. Henry Rainsford died in 1621 at the age of 46, and his lifelong friend Drayton, composed his elegy: *Upon the Death of His Incomparable Friend, Past all Degrees that Was so Deere to Me.*

Anne continued to live at Clifford Chambers through her widowhood, and Drayton continued to spend much of his time with her there. He stayed for the last time in the summer of 1631, just a few months before he died in London.

The night before his death, his thoughts were once again of Anne, now a middle-aged matron, but still Drayton's beloved 'Idea'.

'So well I love thee as without thee I
Love nothing. Yf I might chuse I'de rather dye
Than be on(e) day debarde thy companie
So all my thoughts are peyces but of You. . . .'

So died Mr Drayton, that excellent poet. He died poor, as he had lived, and Henry Peacham writing shortly afterwards declared 'Honest Mr Michael Drayton has but five pounds lying by him at his death. . . .' He left no will, but his brother Edmund administered his small 'estate' and all his goods were valued at £24 8s 2d.

He died in a lodging in Fleet Street, but was so well-beloved, we are told, that 'Gentlemen of the Four Inns of Court and others of note about the Towne' attended his body to Westminster where he was buried in the Abbey, faithful to the end to his 'Idea', his beloved Anne.

The old manor house at Clifford Chambers was destroyed by fire in 1918, and was rebuilt, largely on the original plan, by Sir Edward Lutyens, with the gardens by Gertrude Jekyll. In recent years it has been an hotel.

The
Mad Doctor
of Southam

THE National Health Service of which we are so proud in this country began just after the end of the Second World War, but a small Warwickshire village had its own health service, organised by a caring parish doctor, as long ago as 1818 and it ran very successfully. So successfully, in fact, that many important people came to have a look at it, and then went back to try to get some kind of similar scheme started in their own area.

It was the noble idea of Henry Lilley Smith, who was born in Southam in 1787, and as a young man served as military surgeon to the 45th Regiment with Sir John Moore at Corunna. He obtained his MRCS in 1810 and returned to his native Southam, where he was appointed parish surgeon.

He was a dedicated man, with ideas far in advance of his time, and he was one of the early, even perhaps one of the original, members of the Provincial Medical and Surgical Association (now the British Medical Association) and served on the Council of that august body.

Once back home in Southam, his adventuring days over, Dr Smith set about putting many of his pet schemes into operation. The first of these was the opening of a small hospital dealing mainly with diseases of the eye and ear, which he had noted were particularly prevalent among the poor and labour-

ing classes. This building was on land adjoining his own house, and was supported entirely by voluntary subscriptions. Patients were admitted from quite far afield, and many were treated as outpatients as well. The medical advice and the medicine were entirely free of charge, but a small sum of a few pence was asked if the patient had to be admitted into the hospital. This was to cover the cost of their food during their stay.

Dr Smith was supported in this venture by Sir Grey Skipwith, the local Member of Parliament, and the first patients were admitted in the spring of 1818. Even a far-sighted pioneer needs some support, and Dr Smith's ideas did not receive universal approval. There was quite a lot of prejudice, and many people thought him nothing but a 'meddler'.

However, when the hospital was plainly a success, and the wagging tongues stopped, Dr Smith decided to move on to the next project.

He was not satisfied that medical assistance was as available to the poor as it should be, so his next venture was to establish a self-supporting dispensary, in a small thatched cottage, close to his own home and to his eye and ear infirmary. This was to be run by a committee, and Sir Grey Skipwith agreed to lead it.

Membership was confined to those persons living in or around Southam, and who could not afford to pay for medical advice in the normal way of things. Thus was an income level indirectly fixed.

The annual subscription, paid quarterly or in a lump sum, was 3/6d for adults and 2/- for children. Midwifery was not included in the service. Visits to patients within Southam were free, but for visits further afield a small charge was made.

Dr Smith's consulting hours at this dispensary were 7 am until 10 am on Sundays, and 7 am until noon on Mondays and Thursdays. In addition, he had his own practice, and his infirmary to deal with.

The idea of this dispensary was not unlike that operated in the National Health Service today, and it was a great help to

many poor families. In no time, not only was it self-supporting, it showed a small profit. The only time it failed to do this
was during the cholera epidemic of 1832 when each member
was asked (not required, just asked) to pay an additional 6d
because the services of the dispensary had been so greatly
overworked as this dread disease spread through the town.

You might think that having worked so hard and got this
far, Dr Smith would be satisfied, but he was not. He had
already begun to help the physical condition and the health of
the poor, but he was one of the first to realise that this in itself
was not enough. Recreation was of great importance in the
health and well-being of any individual. In Dr Smith's time
the standard of amusements available to ordinary people was
very low, and there was a lot of drunkenness.

Therefore, in 1825, Dr Smith provided for and arranged a
maypole feast, with music, sports, children dancing around
the maypole and a tea. Everyone was encouraged and indeed
expected to play their part, and the whole event was greatly
enjoyed. So much so that it remained a feature of Southam's
life and continued long after the good doctor died.

The British Medical Association had their eye on Dr Smith
and his *avant garde* ideas though, and he was called to a
special meeting of the Association in 1856 to explain how his
infirmary and his dispensary worked. He was subjected to
extensive criticism, but he was a moderate man, who firmly
believed in all he did, and he met all arguments from the
Association with 'remarkable evenness of temper. . . .' and
carried on doing what he was doing.

Next, Dr Smith turned his attention to youth. The provision
of allotments for labourers had been a contentious issue in the
area, and one in which Dr Smith decided not to meddle. But
he provided allotments for boys, making a parcel of his own
land available for youngsters between the ages of eight and 14.
The rent of each patch of land was 6d a month for nine
months of the year, excluding the winter.

Again, he was called the 'Mad Doctor' but again he per-
sisted, and proved just how successful his ideas could be. After

Southam, he acquired a piece of land at nearby Harbury, and instigated the same scheme with equal success.

The 'Boys Allotments' achieved considerable publicity, and once again notable people visited Southam to see how it all worked, and found to their astonishment that it worked very well indeed. The young boys had something to interest themselves in, and the doctor took a personal interest in their efforts.

One thing leads to another; when the boys came filing up to the doctor's back door to pay their rent, he realised that there was a considerable dearth of reading matter in the average labourer's cottage. Many of the boys could read, albeit not especially well, but how were they to improve themselves without books?

Dr Smith collected together a library of books he considered suitable reading for his allotment boys; good stories, some religious, all highly moral, and with a few of the swashbuckling adventures that boys of that age and era loved. When the boys called with their rent, they were allowed to borrow one book, and were required to return it on the next rent day.

During the whole of his lifetime in his native town, Dr Smith worked tirelessly to improve the conditions he saw around him. He helped with advice when people in other towns sought to emulate his ideas. His dispensary remained successful and took up a great amount of his time. It flourished until the good doctor himself died in 1859. The building was used for some time by his successor, but was eventually demolished as unsafe.

In 1889, the Rev William Smith, son of Dr Henry Lilley Smith, presented to the town of Southam a stone monument, erected on the site of his father's dispensary. However, after a few years the land upon which this monument stood had to be sold, and the edifice was removed to its present position. A financial bequest from the family ensures it remains there.

It is a lasting tribute to the work of Dr Smith, a man of both ideas and ideals, who instead of wringing his hands, used them to better the lot of his fellow men.

The King's Favourite

IT was at Blacklow Hill, not far from the county town of Warwick, that the brutal execution took place in 1312 of the King's 'favourite', the Gascon, Piers Gaveston.

The Barons had long since tired of the foolishness of the King, Edward II, who came to the throne upon the death of his father in 1307. The weaknesses which had already shown themselves in Edward when he was Prince of Wales, were given full rein in him as King. His wanton lasciviousness disgusted most of his court, and especially Guy Beauchamp, Earl of Warwick.

Edward was given to making favourites of the most unsuitable people, not because of their service to the throne, but because of their ability to entertain him and enter with him into devious debaucheries. Piers Gaveston was one of these.

He was, by all accounts, a most beautiful young man. His features were of a classic nobility, his eyes soft and dark, his forehead broad and intellectual, crowned with masses of dark wavy hair. His teeth, we are told, were 'as white as egg shells'. He had a brilliant sparkling wit and intellect, and he had early absorbed all the romanticism of the Gascon troubadours.

All who met him fell instantly beneath his immense charm, but it soon palled upon closer acquaintance, when it became all too obvious that the young man was cruel, and took sensual pleasure in being so. Together with the King, the young man pursued every vice available, and their behaviour shocked even that bloodstained age.

The Gascon had been brought to England by the old King to act as a companion to his son, but when he began to exhibit his true character, the old King banished him. One of the first things Edward II did was to fetch him back to the court, to make him a favourite, and to enact vengeance upon all those whom he considered had a hand in Gaveston's banishment. He found a rich wife for the Gascon, and married him to Margaret, daughter of Gilbert de Clare, the King's Consul, and a very unhappy time that lady had in her marriage.

The King showered gifts upon his beloved 'Perot' as he called Gaveston, even giving him jewels belonging to the Queen herself, Isabel of France, and thus shaming her before the court. He gave him a table and a pair of trestles made of solid gold, treasured heirlooms of England, believed to have once belonged to the great King Arthur.

The Barons rumbled and grumbled, and complained bitterly to the King, but to no avail. The King and the Gascon delighted in paying them back every time they spoke against 'Perot'.

Eventually the scandal grew so great that the King was forced to send Gaveston to Ireland. But he then proceeded to send him so many expensive gifts, that the Barons decided it was cheaper to have him back here under their eye, and so he returned.

His arrogance then knew no bounds, and he instantly made an enemy of the great Earl of Warwick by dubbing him 'the black hound of Arden'. Guy Beauchamp growled that one day the Gascon should 'feel the teeth of the black hound'. The King and his favourite jibed at the Earls and nobles, and the Barons plotted together.

In 1312 the King left Gaveston behind at Scarborough. It was not long before the Barons realised their opportunity, and joining forces they marched to Scarborough and laid siege to Gaveston, ensconced within his castle. He was no match for them without the King to back him up, and he surrendered to them on their promise to spare his life and take him back to London.

They did march towards London, and at Deddington, on the Warwickshire/Oxfordshire border, they rested for a night, putting their prisoner in the old rectory house, with the Earl of Pembroke to keep guard over him. However, leaving a few retainers, the Earl decided to pay a conjugal visit to his wife who was in the neighbourhood. Whether this was entirely innocent, or whether this was all part of the plot, no one has ever discovered, but the Earl of Warwick pounced.

'I have come to keep my vow', said the great Earl, and Gaveston knew he was doomed to feel the 'hound's teeth'. Dragged from his bed, bemused with sleep, the Gascon was rushed towards Warwick Castle.

There in the Great Hall he was forced to stand rough trial by the assembled Barons, all of whom, smarting from his jokes and jibes at their expense, wished him dead. The trial was a mockery; Gaveston's charm and wit, the mental agility that had so delighted the King, stood him in no stead before these determined and ruthless men of war.

He threw himself on their mercy, and it is just possible that he might have lighted some spark of clemency, until a voice from the back of the room was heard to shout 'You have caught the Fox. If you let him go now, you will have to hunt him all over again'.

Gaveston was dragged screaming to nearby Blacklow Hill, in the dark hours of the early morning of the 19th June, 1312, and there he was without ceremony savagely beheaded. His head is said to have rolled beneath a furze bush, from which it was subsequently retrieved by an itinerant friar. Some of the brethren from Greyfriars, Oxford, later came and took the discarded body back for Christian burial. Two years later, on the King's orders, it was once more removed and given a funeral of great pomp, with cloth of gold, and reinterred in the King's own land at King's Langley, Hertfordshire.

Strange to relate, all involved in this lawless act themselves met violent deaths within the ensuing few years. The Earl of Lancaster was brutally done to death in Pontefract Castle, the Earl of Pembroke was stabbed to death by a paid killer, and the Earl of Arundel was beheaded. Guy Beauchamp, Earl of Warwick, did die in his own bed, but in agony from poison administered by an adherent of Gaveston, in revenge.

Edward II was finally forced to leave the throne he had occupied with such great dishonour, and was for a time kept at Kenilworth Castle, Warwickshire, by Roger Mortimer, Queen Isabel's lover. In 1327 the King was taken to Berkeley Castle in Gloucestershire, and most foully, cruelly and bestially murdered.

The land upon which Blacklow Hill stands subsequently came into the ownership of Mr Bertie Greatheed, a man with an abiding interest in the history of our Shires. In 1821 he erected a stone monument to commemorate the execution of Piers Gaveston, and he got his friend, Dr Samuel Parr, the eccentric and scholarly vicar of nearby Hatton, to compose the inscription:

'In the hollow of this rock was beheaded in the first day of July 1312 by barons lawless as himself, Piers Gaveston, Earl of Cornwall, the minion of a hateful king, in life and death a memorable instance of misrule.'

Strangely, considering Dr Parr's undoubted and renowned scholarship, he got the date wrong. The difference between the Old Style calendar and the New Style calendar in 1312, was only eight days, but the inscription makes the variation amount to twelve days, which is the difference between the Old and the New at the time the monument was erected.

The event is also commemorated in a slightly more popular fashion on an inn sign in Southam, 'The Black Dog'. The board does not bear the canine representation you might expect, but instead it pictures the group of barons at the beheading, and beyond waves the banner of Gaveston's 'black dog' – the great Earl of Warwick.

The Warwickshire Princess

Dr James Wilmot, Doctor of Divinity, bookworm and bachelor, became rector of the tiny village of Barton-on-the-Heath in 1782, and moved into the rambling old rectory accompanied by a lively little girl, whom everyone assumed to be his niece, Olive, the daughter of his brother Robert.

Imagine their astonishment, therefore, when some years later this little girl, now a middle-aged woman, claimed to be the Princess Olive, daughter of Prince Henry Frederick, Duke of Cumberland. Olive's own daughter brought a celebrated case at law petitioning that her mother be declared legitimate and of the Blood Royal, that she herself might receive her rightful dues, and that her son should be declared a legitimate descendant of King George II.

By this time, of course, Dr Wilmot was dead and buried, and could not be called upon to verify the truth of the many fairly outrageous statements made by Olive and her circle.

Olive was about ten when she went to live at Barton-on-the-Heath, and was known as 'little Miss Wilmot'. She was a very pretty child, but had a wild streak in her which caused her to behave very badly at times, not at all like a demure little Miss from a rectory. Her great delight in her teenage years was to get into the rector's library in his absence and read therein all those books usually kept out of the reach of growing young ladies.

Perhaps her reading put ideas into her head, for she was involved in many unlikely escapades during the rector's absences. One in particular landed her in court as a witness.

It was in the winter of 1790 when Olive would be about 18 years old. A local farmer trudging through heavy snow at Barton-on-the-Heath to check up on his sheep was considerably taken aback when he saw before him the lithe, lissom figure of 'little Miss Wilmot', stark naked except for a brief shawl, loping barefoot across the snow.

Olive, obviously equally taken aback to find someone else abroad this early in the day, filled him up with a tearful story of having escaped the house with her life when it was broken into by robbers in her uncle's absence. The farmer wrapped the young woman in his coat and took her back to his own home where his wife found something for her to wear, and gave her warm food. Gathering up a few stalwart farmhands, the farmer trooped back to the rectory where he found the few servants tied up and gagged, and the house in a great deal of a mess.

When they were released however, the servants looked askance at Olive, and it was revealed that on the previous evening, after her uncle was safely out of the way, she had gone out of the front door and fired a loaded shotgun. There being no other explanation, the servants believed their young mistress had signalled to the ruffians that the master was safely out of the way and the coast was clear. The authorities believed Olive's story of her innocence, but nobody else did!

By this time Olive Wilmot had developed a talent for both writing and painting, writing a few romantic stories, and producing some pleasing small landscapes. She had grown into a beauty, with great charm and fascination. She was also unscrupulous, determined to get her own way, totally selfish, hedonistic, and 'economical with the truth'.

Her behaviour at Barton-on-the-Heath continued to shock, so the good Dr Wilmot took her to London to live with his brother, where he perhaps hoped to get her married off, or at least find sufficient occupation to keep her out of mischief.

It was not long before the beautiful Miss Wilmot met and married Royal Marine painter John Serres. They had two surviving daughters, Lavinia and Britannia, and John Serres, with a fellow artist called George Field, began the British School of Artists.

The marriage was a stormy one, with Olive romping through the money faster than it came in, and in 1804 a legal deed of separation was drawn up between them. Olive handed the children over to almost anyone who would take them, and launched herself on her own career both as a writer and painter. Under the name Mrs Olive Wilmot Serres, she published *Flights of Fancy*, *St Julian* and the *Castle of Avalon* in rapid succession, and was appointed landscape painter to the Prince of Wales.

During the years up to 1813 Olive was also engaged in scandal, blackmail, writing begging letters, and various other unsavoury matters!

Sometime around the year 1817, Olive declared herself to be a Princess of the Blood Royal, the legitimate daughter of King George III's brother the Duke of Cumberland, and she adopted the royal arms, livery and seals used by junior members of the Royal Family. She insisted on being called 'Royal Highness', and came up with an amazing story, which eventually would reach its final conclusion in the courts in 1866.

The Wilmots were a Warwick family, and claimed descent from the Earl of Rochester, the witty buffoon of Charles II's court. Be that as it may, as far as could be seen in the 18th century, the head of the family was Thomas Wilmot, who had married a woman called Sarah, and together they kept a pub in Warwick. They had three children: Olive, who married a soldier, Captain William Payne; Robert, who married Anna-Maria; and James. James, the good Dr Wilmot of Barton-on-the-Heath, went to Oxford and became a scholar, becoming Doctor of Divinity in 1769.

It was alleged that while James Wilmot was up at Oxford, he met and married the Princess Poniatowski, sister to the King of Poland. They married secretly in 1749 and the following year a daughter was born and baptised Olive.

The Doctor kept his marriage secret, since as a Fellow of his College he would not have been allowed to marry. No information has ever come to light about the Princess Poniatowski, and we do not hear of her again.

In 1767, Dr Wilmot visited Lord Archer at his house in Grosvenor Square, taking with him his daughter Olive, aged 17. Also visiting Lord Archer was young Prince Henry Frederick, the 22 year old Duke of Cumberland. The young man fell head over heels in love with the beautiful Olive, and shortly afterwards they were married with Olive's father, Dr Wilmot, performing the ceremony.

They lived together in perfect happiness, until for some quite undisclosed reason, the Duke went off and married Lady Anne Luttrell. It seems his brother the King knew nothing of either marriage, and was so put out that he rushed through the Royal Marriage Act, which forbade any of the Royal Family under 25 years of age to marry without the Sovereign's consent, without further delay.

Upon hearing the news that her husband, the Prince, had married another woman, Olive fled to her grandmother's house in Warwick, where she gave birth to a daughter, also baptised Olive.

During the same month of the same year, Dr Wilmot's brother Robert also had a daughter, baptised Olive! Robert Wilmot was known locally as 'Black Bob', because having obtained a lucrative job as county treasurer, he had immediately disappeared with the rate money!

So who was Olive – our 'little Miss Wilmot'? Was she the daughter of Black Bob, and in reality Dr Wilmot's niece, whom he sought to educate in the rectory at Barton-on-the-Heath? Or was she really his own grand-daughter? The tale is nothing if not confusing!

Olive continued to pass herself off as a Princess in London.

She drove in a coach with the Royal arms, and she is alleged to have been visited by the Royal brothers, to whom she showed proof of her birth, and received their welcome as a royal niece.

But none of it did her much good. She was constantly in debt and ultimately it was in the Fleet prison that she died in 1834.

Her daughter Lavinia Ryves brought the court case in 1866. She had by this time acquired a philandering husband and six children, and lived in St Pancras in very modest circumstances verging upon poverty.

She trotted out all the 'evidence', and produced all the papers prepared by her mother, which numbered more than a hundred. The court ruled that the documents should be impounded, and said that they were not satisfied with the claims of the 'Princess'. In other words, they did not believe a word of it! The case was over.

Olive Wilmot was probably one of the most colourful imposters of all time. It seems that the 'Warwickshire Maid' (the words of the Earl of Warwick) was just that, and not a real 'Warwickshire Princess' after all.

Of
Apparitions
and Spectres

WARWICKSHIRE has its fair share of ghostly manifestations. Indeed, so many are there it seems incredible that anyone can make their way along any street or lane without bumping into countless monks, nuns and grey ladies, or being run down by phantom coaches!

The hills which cushion the verdant village of Ilmington, eight miles south of Stratford-on-Avon, are well populated with ghosts. The most spectacular is the night hunt, with a pack of spectral hounds streaming across the hills, led by a ghostly huntsman. The story is that there was once a man living in Ilmington who loved nothing so much as hunting. So keen and eager was he that he kept and maintained his own pack. One day he was forced to travel elsewhere on a matter of business, and had to miss a day's hunting. He hurriedly got the business finished with and rode home again, even though by this time darkness had fallen, and he would have done better to seek a lodging for the night.

As he neared home, he heard his hounds baying. They too had missed the day's sport. Nothing loath, he rode down to their kennels to greet them, for he was fond of the creatures. But, as I said, it was dark. The hounds had been deprived not only of their day in the field, but of their prey as well. When

their master dismounted and opened the gate to go in among them, they fell upon him and tore him to pieces.

He it is who leads the ghostly hunt across the Ilmington hills, and should anyone chance to see it, they had best avert their eyes, for to look the huntsman in the face is to put yourself forever in his power.

A phantom coach with a headless driver seated on the box rushes headlong from the direction of the village of Mickleton nearby, through Ilmington, and out the other side. There is another coach too where not only the driver is minus his head, but so are all six horses! This story relates to a quarrel between neighbours.

It appears that a Mr Canning who lived at Foxcote was at loggerheads with a Captain Barnsley, who owned the adjoining estate. The men quarrelled over many things, the last one being which of them had the most game upon his land. They agreed to meet for a duel, but before the appointed date, they came face to face once again as they walked, each on their own land.

Harsh words followed, and Canning, who had a staff in his hand, killed Barnsley in the heat of the moment, then promptly fled to France. It is Captain Barnsley who rides inside the coach with the headless horses, all the time combing the Ilmington hills, searching for Canning and for vengeance.

The result of all this ghostly traffic has been to set the bells of the church ringing with no one there to pull on the ropes. 'To frighten off the Devil', say the Ilmington folks.

Bedworth, in the north of the county has a phantom funeral procession which wends its way through Wootton Street on winter mornings. The cortege with its black plumed horses and turn-of-the-century trappings, always moves at a pace appropriate to a funeral, and yet no one who sees it can ever catch up with it, even if they break into a run!

Astley Castle, not far from Nuneaton, is nothing much now, only a romantic ruin, but it has two Very Important People as its ghosts. Little Lady Jane Grey, queen for nine days, lived here before she married into the ill-fated Dudleys, and she may still be spied, flitting through her old home. Her father too, Henry Grey, Duke of Suffolk, foolish and misguided man, fled back to his estate at Astley after his daughter and son-in-law lost their heads, and he himself had been involved in insurrection. Here he remained hidden, securely tucked within a hollow tree. A keeper, knowing him from his former days of affluence, helped him and brought him food. But alas, the lure of the reward proved too big a temptation for the keeper, and for gold he betrayed his master, who was dragged from his hiding place and subsequently executed. His headless spectre appears from time to time where the old hollow oak once stood.

The tiny village of Idlicote near Shipston-on-Stour has the ghost of a hand-wringing squire, William Underhill. It was this Underhill who sold New Place, Stratford-on-Avon, to William Shakespeare, and through all records he is ever referred to as 'covetous and crafty'. He lived at Idlicote, and his sale of New Place apparently greatly displeased his eldest son, Fulke, who probably wanted to live there himself. Fulke was a bit hot-tempered and he decided he would wait no longer for his inheritance; so he killed his father, by poison.

But he didn't get away with it. He was found out, sent for trial at Warwick, and hanged. Both father and son are buried in the tiny churchyard at Idlicote, but on a summer night, on the anniversary of his untimely death, William Underhill rises from his unquiet grave, and wanders up and down, crying aloud 'My son . . . my son . . . my son. . . .'

At Chadshunt, between Kineton and Gaydon, another squire haunts the scene of his former splendours. The Newshams lived at Chadshunt House for almost three centuries, but then as inevitably happens, the young man who came into the inheritance wasn't up to the mark. He preferred gambling to anything, and so he squandered his considerable fortune until he was compelled to mortgage his house and all his estate at Chadshunt. He lost the lot. Remorsefully he drives his coach and four with a flourish on the drive of the home he once owned.

Ragley Hall, the superb Palladian home of the Marquess of Hertford, near Alcester, has no ghosts within its portals, but a beautiful (and thirsty) lady outside. It seems that in about 1830 the ancient skeleton of a woman was discovered close by a natural spring. It is said she still wanders at night near the place of her burial, and drinks from the spring.

Not far from Ragley Hall is the Arrow Mill, now a restaurant. The lands at Arrow used to belong to the Burdett family, who were quite powerful in Warwickshire at one time. In 1477, Thomas Burdett was particularly proud of a white buck that roamed around his park at Arrow. Alas for poor Thomas, the King (Edward IV) decided upon a whim to go hunting in Burdett's park at Arrow in Thomas's absence. In the course of the day, he shot and killed the white buck.

This so enraged Thomas Burdett that he cried aloud he wished the buck had first sunk its horns in the King's belly! He was overheard, and enemies reported his words to the King, who promptly had him arraigned for treason and beheaded.

Now the white buck still roams Arrow park, pursued by the head of Thomas Burdett.

Wootton Hall, between Stratford-on-Avon and Henley-in-Arden, was once the much-loved home of Viscount Carrington, who fought on the Royalist side in the Civil War. After Naseby, he fled to exile in France accompanied by a valet, and took refuge in Pontoise, where his valet promptly murdered him for his money. The guilty man was caught and paid the penalty for his crime. The heart and viscera of Carrington were brought back to England and buried in a secret chamber at Wootton Hall, the home he loved so well and was cruelly forced to leave. Now, it is said, he never leaves it, nor will he ever have to again, for his ghost is happy there.

A grey lady haunts the site of the old church at Pillerton Priors. This building was inexplicably burned to the ground in 1666, and in no time at all, traces of the building were removed. Local people are notoriously thrifty and saw no reason to leave good stone unused. The churchyard, however, remains to this day, and it is here that the wraith of the grey lady may be seen flitting between the overgrown and untended graves.

The Blue Lias Inn at Stockton, near Southam, is haunted by the ghost of a good-looking red-haired young man. It appears the young man was a labourer who had a way with the ladies. The Blue Lias was at one time a farmhouse; the farmer was often away from home, and his young wife got lonely. The labourer was only too ready to console her. The master returned unexpectedly one night, and discovered the two of them together, and so he killed the red-headed young man in a fit of righteous anger. In remorse, the young man remains to haunt the Blue Lias Inn.

It is a rascally old miller that haunts the hill near Bearley, north of Stratford-on-Avon. A mill once stood upon this land, and the miserly man overcharged the poor people for grinding their corn. He made a very great deal of money in this way, but he never spent any of it. Instead he stored it in sacks beneath the stone floor. Nothing is left there now, but the ghost of the old miller haunts the spot, to prevent anyone ever finding out where he hid his gold.

In Haseley Park, not far from Warwick, is a haunted pond, from whose still waters on a moonlit night rises the wraith of Sir Thomas Charlecote, once lord of this manor. The poor man was murdered by three of his servants, and his body flung into the pond, sometime in 1263. When the body was eventually recovered, it was assumed that Sir Thomas had committed suicide by drowning himself in his own pond. His goods and lands therefore were forfeit to the Crown. But the truth will out. Sir Thomas was found to have been strangled not drowned, and his murderers were eventually brought to justice, tried and hanged. Sir Thomas's heirs were able to receive back their inheritance from the Crown.

The ghost of a lovelorn and languishing curate haunts the church he once served at Little Compton, the southernmost village in Warwickshire. The story has it that this young man fell in love with a lady with a beautiful voice who sang every

Sunday in his church choir. But the young lady aimed somewhat higher than a mere curate, and became betrothed to the
owner of the Grange! This heartless and insensitive young
woman then insisted that the marriage should take place in
Little Compton church, with the young curate himself officiat-
ing at the ceremony. It broke the young man's heart, but he
did perform the service. After watching the happy couple
leave the church, he disappeared, only to be found later that
same day hanging from a bell rope.

A ghost bicycle is slightly more unusual, but there is a ghost
cyclist complete with ancient machine in the village of Stone-
leigh. This spectre cycles wildly downhill with a look of
apprehension upon his face, and then disappears into a stone
wall. It is thought to be the ghost of a man who was killed in a
cycling accident on this spot in the 1880s.

A stretch of the main A34 Stratford-on-Avon to Oxford
road is haunted by the ghost of a man murdered by high-
waymen. Seeking to rob him, they killed him instead and
flung his body into a gravel pit that used to serve the village of
Clifford Chambers, from where he emerges every now and
again.

An old woman in a sun-bonnet with a basket on her arm
walks the same main road, only a few miles further on towards
Tredington.

At Pillerton Hersey they have a screeching gypsy, who has
given her name to the coppice in which she lived and died.
Poor Moll was slightly mad, and was suspected of witchcraft.
Everything that went wrong in the neighbourhood was blamed
on Moll, who was in the habit of wandering among the trees
screeching like an owl. In desperation, and in madness, poor
Moll killed herself and was buried where two bridle paths
cross in the woods. This coppice is to this day known as
Mollsgrave Coppice, and there are still those who believe the
screech of owls may well be the ghost of Mad Moll.

The
Kidnapped
Bridegroom

USUALLY in stories of kidnappings, lost love and elope-ments, it is the young girl who has been whisked off by her lover or her lover's family. But in the case of Alice and John, it was entirely the reverse.

The Bracebridge family was an old and honourable one, who settled in Warwickshire when Peter de Bracebridge came from Lincoln to Warwick to be married to the beautiful Alicia, granddaughter of Turchill, Sheriff of Warwickshire. They took as their seat Kingsbury Hall at the northern end of the county, and here on land overlooking the river Tame, they settled, built, fortified, flourished and prospered.

In the 15th century, the heiress of the Bracebridge family was Alice, fair of face, very young, dreamy and romantic, and the apple of her ageing father's eye.

Next door to the Bracebridges stood Park Hall, the home of the Ardens, an ancient family of higher status; a family full of pride, who owned vast estates, and who always sought by judicious marriages to improve themselves still further. Com-pared to the Ardens, the Bracebridges were comparative newcomers. And all the current hopes of the Ardens were centred on their eldest son, and the heir, John Arden.

John Arden and Alice Bracebridge fell in love, and this didn't go down well with either family. The Ardens looked for a much more high-flown union than this for their son, and Richard Bracebridge was inclined to consider the Ardens a bit soft, and would have preferred a more soldier-like husband for his daughter.

The young couple were forbidden to see each other. John was confined to the family estate, and Alice wandered around the bounds of Kingsbury Hall. John was miserable; Alice pined.

The amiable river Tame ran through both the adjoining estates, and John would drop wild flowers onto its shining waters, hoping they would be gathered up by Alice as they were carried through the meadows of Kingsbury Hall. Alice did indeed gather up the sodden blossoms, knowing John had picked them.

Richard Bracebridge was devoted to his daughter, and as she wandered aimlessly around, he hated to think of her so unhappy; he feared for her health since she grew more and more wan and pale. He wondered why John Arden did not take more positive steps to woo and win his love, but the cautious side of his nature realised that in so doing, John could well lose his inheritance. To Richard Bracebridge, inheritance was of considerable importance, just as it was to the Ardens.

However, he began to find Alice's tears and sighs very wearing, and eventually he decided he could bear it no longer.

Early one morning, before the houehold was astir, he called together a few trusty retainers, and together they rode towards Park Hall. It was a simple matter to capture John Arden from beneath his parents' noses, and to ride off with him back to Kingsbury Hall. John put up no resistance, and allowed himself to be handed over to Alice, who instantly stopped sighing and weeping, to the great relief of all around her.

John Arden remained a complacent and happy prisoner within the strong fortified walls of Kingsbury Hall, while his parents lamented their lot at Park Hall. To abduct a daughter was bad enough, heaven knows, but to make off with a son and heir was unthinkable. The Ardens went to law; to the

Lords of the land, and right up to the King, Edward IV himself, demanding justice, restitution and compensation.

The Lords debated at length, but the young couple happy at last in each other's company, didn't really care what was being said on either side. The lengthy legal battle waged above their heads.

Eventually a decision was reached. The pair were to be married in February 1474, and Alice was to have 200 marks settled upon her as her jointure. Richard Bracebridge was severely reprimanded for his trespass, and ordered to give Walter Arden, John's father, the best horse that could be found from the Kingsbury Hall stables.

Ultimately, as in all good stories, the Ardens and the Bracebridges became better friends, and when Walter Arden died in 1502, Richard Bracebridge was the executor of his will.

John and Alice settled down to comfortable wedlock, and founded the Staffordshire branch of the Arden family. John's younger brother settled at Wilmcote, near Stratford-on-Avon, and became the great-grandfather of William Shakespeare.

The Laurel Water Murder

LAWFORD Hall, near Little Lawford, about two miles from Rugby in Warwickshire, has long since been razed to the ground, and no trace remains of this once beautiful mansion, seat of the Boughton family. It was considered a 'thing accursed', for it was the scene of a dastardly murder which set the whole county by the ears.

It was the first and only case where laurel water is known to have been used to poison, and as such is unique in the annals of crime. Warwickshire has the doubtful distinction of being the venue.

The story began innocently enough. In 1777 the Dowager Lady Boughton of Lawford Hall, accompanied her young daughter to fashionable Bath, where they were to take the waters for the benefit of their health, and to enjoy a season in that fashionable spa. The town was exceptionally full when they arrived and there were no rooms to be had anywhere. Mother and daughter were forced to spend their first night in the town sitting on chairs in the coffee room of an inn, the only accommodation the harrassed landlord could find for them.

But there was a gallant and dashing young officer staying at this same inn, and when he heard the plight of the two ladies, what else could he do, but instantly gave up his room to their use. The Dowager was relieved and gratified, and graciously invited the officer to join them for breakfast.

Captain John Donnellan, of Irish birth, a subaltern of the 39th regiment, on half-pay and trying to supplement his meagre resources by gambling, was a charmer. He was good-looking, with impeccable manners, witty conversation and a touch of the Irish blarney. In less time than it takes to trim a whisker, both the Dowager and her daughter had fallen beneath his spell. Particularly the daughter.

Miss Boughton was very young, and had had a sheltered upbringing as befitted the daughter of the wealthy Boughtons. Never before had she met anyone like the gallant Captain, and her head was quite turned. Captain Donnellan, whose upbringing had *not* been sheltered, saw his golden opportunity and seized it. He paid excessive court to little Miss Boughton, paid her extravagant compliments, sent her flowers, bought her suitable gifts, and was ready to escort her and the Dowager to wherever they wished to go. He was concerned with their comfort, and was able to plan many small and simple excursions to make their stay pleasurable. Miss Boughton's head was filled with romantic notions and the Captain figured largely in all of them.

The Captain was, however, no fool. He realised that he would not be considered at all a suitable match for the wealthy and sheltered Miss Boughton, and that any such suggestion on his part would merely cause her family to rush her home and to remove her for ever from his sight.

The outcome was inevitable: Captain Donnellan and the giddy little Miss Boughton eloped, to the intense rage of the Boughton family, who took no time in branding the Captain a common fortune hunter.

However, the knot was well and truly legally tied, and they could do little about it, but were slightly mollified when Captain Donnellan unexpectedly agreed to forego any share in his wife's fortune, now or in the future.

Just a year after their clandestine marriage, the couple returned to make their home at Lawford Hall. Unfortunately, this event coincided with the return of Sir Theodosius Bough-ton, Mrs Donnellan's brother, who had left Eton and decided to take up his role of Warwickshire squire, with the family, at Lawford Hall.

Sir Theodosius was a singularly unpleasant young man, thoroughly spoiled by his foolish, doting, widowed mother, and allowed to squander far too much money. Whilst at Eton he had indulged in every vice available to him, and when these ran out, he invented a few of his own. Now, at 20 years of age, he was sickly, belligerent, contrary, cruel and totally unlikeable.

He detested Captain Donnellan on sight, although at first the Captain did seem to be trying to make a friend out of his brother-in-law, to take an interest in his activities, and to try to like him. He showed concern over the baronet's poor health, but the baronet failed to appreciate any of it.

On 21st August 1780, a Lawford Hall servant was sent to collect a bottle of medicine for the young baronet. It was an ordinary enough mixture of rhubarb and jalap, prescribed for the young man by his physician on numerous previous occasions. The servant handed the bottle to Sir Theo on his return to the Hall, and this was the last the man saw of it.

Sir Theo took it into his head to go fishing in the lake, despite the chill and the damp, and the same servant was ordered to accompany him. Captain Donnellan, seemingly worried about his brother-in-law taking yet another chill, tried to persuade him to give up the idea and return to the house, but Sir Theo obstinately refused, becoming quite abusive in the process.

On the following morning, the Dowager went into her son's room, as was her doting custom, to arouse Sir Theo. As soon as he was awake, she promptly administered a dose of the medicine which was standing on the night table by the bed. Sir Theo grumblingly gulped it down, and then complained that it tasted bitter, was more unpleasant than usual and made him feel sick.

In a matter of moments, the young man was obviously in

desperate agony. He was convulsed and contorted, his teeth were clenched and froth and saliva were being forced through his tight lips. In a panic, the Dowager screamed for help and sent a servant to fetch the doctor with all possible speed.

Hearing the shouts and the commotion, Captain Donnellan came running into the sick room, but he scarce spared a glance for the figure writhing and mouthing upon the bed. Ignoring everything else, he hurried to the night table, grabbed the medicine bottle and the glass which had contained the dose, and hurried out with them before anyone could stop him. Not that anyone tried; all eyes were on Sir Theodosius, whose agonies and convulsions were horrific. By the time the doctor arrived, the Baronet had breathed his last.

Later, however, the Captain's extraordinary behaviour caused comment, especially among the Lawford Hall servants. None of them held the dead Sir Theo in any affection, but they all found it odd that the Captain should show no sorrow upon seeing the young man dying, but should be more concerned with removing a bottle and glass.

The Captain meanwhile was at pains to point out to all and sundry that he had not even been in the room when the young baronet was taken ill.

There was a great deal of talk about a post-mortem. Several doctors were called to Lawford Hall to examine the body, but apparently left without doing so. Eventually, the remains of the unlikeable Sir Theodosius were sealed in a lead coffin and buried without further ado.

But that was not the end of it. Rumour and suspicion grew rife and at length an exhumation was ordered. Several doctors of repute carried out a belated post-mortem, and discovered Sir Theodosius had been poisoned with deadly laurel water.

A book of poisons and their use was found in Captain Donnellan's room and, carelessly, the page dealing with the making and administering of laurel water had been marked by turning down the corner. Captain Donnellan was charged with the wilful murder of his brother-in-law, the young baronet, and a close-meshed net of evidence closed in around him.

The trial, which lasted for some time, caused a great stir. The Captain loudly protested his innocence, pointing out that he had nothing to gain by the young man's death since he had already entered into an agreement to forego any part in his wife's fortune. His evidence about his movements on the fateful day, however, was entirely the opposite of the evidence given to the court by the Dowager. Donnellan was found guilty by his peers, and sentenced to be hanged.

While he was languishing in Warwick gaol he advised his young wife to get out of Lawford Hall, and said he believed the Dowager Lady Boughton had poisoned both her son and her husband! To the end the Captain maintained his innocence.

He was hanged at the Saltisford in Warwick early in the morning of 2nd April 1781. The hangman politely apologised to his client for getting him up at such an early hour, but explained he was very busy, and had already had to go to Birmingham to hang two felons that morning before he got to Warwick!

After her husband suffered the extreme penalty, the wealthy young Mrs Donnellan changed her name to Beecham. She subsequently married again, but the two Donnellan children were kept in total ignorance of their parentage, and knew nothing of their father's dire fate. But the truth invariably gets out somehow, and in a young man's squabble over some trifling matter, the boy was taunted by a school friend with being the 'spawn of a murderer'. When he learned the awful truth of this, he hanged himself. The Captain's little daughter died in infancy of natural causes.

Lawford Hall was demolished in 1790. All that is left is the story, believed to be the only murder by this method in the history of crime.

The Legend of Guy of Warwick

MANY tales have been told of the magnificent exploits of Guy of Warwick, our own folk hero, through the ages. According to legend, during the time of Alfred the Great, Rohand was the Earl of Warwick, and he had a beautiful daughter named Phelice. Guy was born at Warwick, the son of Earl Rohand's steward, and from a very early age he gave indications of his great strength, agility and cleverness, so that at the age of 16, Earl Rohand was very pleased to take the young man into his own household. Which is, of course, where he met the fair Phelice.

He fell in love with her, but she would have none of him. Phelice knew better than to waste herself on someone so far beneath her. However, Phelice had a vision in which she was told not to be so unkind to Guy, who had a true heart and a brave soul. Phelice then told Guy that she would love him if he would like to go away and do brave deeds, thus making himself more worthy of her.

So off he went. In Normandy he found a lady called Dorinda who was just about to be burned, and he saved her! He fought her persecutors, and won, and when he got ready to sail back to England, he found they were pursuing him, so he had to stop and fight them all over again.

Then he paused briefly in Germany and took part in a

grand tournament for which the prize was the Emperor's daughter, the Lady Blanche, mounted on a milk-white steed, with greyhounds by her side and a falcon on her wrist.

Well naturally Guy won, but although the Lady Blanche was fair, Guy was constant if nothing else, and declared his love for Phelice. Because he was constant to his love in the romantic tradition, the Lady Blanche shed tears, but bade him return to Phelice and wished him godspeed.

Back came Guy fleet of foot and hot of blood towards Warwick, and the Lady Phelice received him. He told her that he had spurned an Emperor's daughter for her sake, and Phelice was slightly less frosty, but told him that before she would become his wife, he had better go off and do a few more deeds of daring-do to make himself truly worthy of her!

So off went Guy again, and heard of the great Dun Cow which was terrifying everybody and ravaging Dunsmore Heath. The great beast was said to be six yards long and eight yards high, to have eyes of red fire, skin that no blade would penetrate, and horns yards long. All around Dunsmore Heath it had laid waste the crops and buildings and the inhabitants had fled, leaving their hovels to the depredations of the creature.

Guy, mounted on his trusty steed, engaged the monstrous animal in battle. His arrows bounced off her sides, her great horns pierced his armour, but still Guy battled, until he eventually managed to cleave her in the forehead with his huge battleaxe, and the beast faltered and fell. Guy dismounted and struck again and again until with a great surge of blood, the creature died. The overjoyed inhabitants were loud in their praise of their hero, and the ribs of the Dun Cow were despatched to Warwick to be hung in the Great Hall.

There was no end to the valiant deeds performed by Guy. He battled with robbers in the forest and single handed slew 16 of them. He set sail for Byzantium, a city besieged by Turks and Saracens, and all by himself he despatched the marauders and relieved the city.

The giant Colbrand, pagan champion of the Saracens,

challenged our hero to a duel and Guy slew him in battle. He was then instantly challenged by the Saracen Soldan, and he too was rapidly despatched.

Guy's attention was then drawn to a dragon which was bothering the people of a neighbouring village, so once more he lined up to do battle and came off victorious. He returned to England, pausing merely to slay a wild and maddened bear, before rushing off to Northumberland, where he sent another dragon to its ancestors.

He then thought that perhaps he had proved enough, so he returned to Warwick to lay his conquests at the feet of the fair Phelice, who now declared herself satisfied that he was worthy of her. They were married in Warwick amid great feasting and rejoicing. Rohand died, and Guy became Earl by right of his wife, and they had a small son whom they called Reynbourn. Alas, the child was stolen away by foreign mercenaries, and Guy fell into a melancholy.

Guy began thinking of the blood he had shed, and decided that he must make atonement. He once more set sail bent upon a pilgrimage to the Holy Land, and it was some years before he returned.

But although he returned to Warwick, he did not return to Phelice. His appearance was much changed and although that lady, as was her custom, dispensed alms to beggars at the gate of the castle, she did not recognise her own husband among the ragged and starving.

Guy decided to become a hermit and took himself off to live in a cave at the place that is now known as Guy's Cliffe. Here he lived out the rest of his life and the Lady Phelice, believing her lord to have been killed on his pilgrimage, lived alone.

Then Guy fell sick unto death, and knew the end was upon him. Fishing around in his rags, he took a ring from the small pouch he wore at his waist and hailing a passing swineherd, bade him take the ring to the Lady Phelice and ask her to come to him.

The Lady recognising the ring obeyed forthwith, and was just in time to greet her love before Guy closed his eyes in death.

The cave is still there, together with an odd inscription on the wall, in crude Saxon runic characters of the 10th century. It says 'Yd crist-tu icniecti this i-wihtth, Guhthi', which has been translated (by Mr Ralph Carr Ellison in 1870) as 'Cast out thou Christ from thy servant this burden, Guhthi'. Some think that Guthi was the name of a hermit who undoubtedly once lived there. Others have decided its proper translation should be 'Guy'.

A
Double
Murderer

THE old manor house at Baddesley Clinton, not far off the main road between Warwick and Birmingham, is thought to be one of the finest examples of a medieval semi-fortified home to have survived in the Midlands. Hidden from the casual observer, it still manages to enjoy an air of quiet seclusion, although since its acquisition by the National Trust many visitors make their way to it across the woodland paths.

Much of the original house built by John Brome around 1459 still remains, although it has been added to by various occupiers since.

Close by stands the little parish church, dedicated to St James for most of its life, but changed to St Michael's when it was restored in 1872. It owes its tower and peal of bells to Nicholas Brome, son of the builder of Baddesley Clinton Hall. And thereby hangs a dark tale of murder.

The Bromes were a prominent Warwickshire family in the 15th and 16th centuries, and are believed to have originated and taken their name from Brome Hall, once a moated manor near Lapworth.

John Brome was a burgess of the town of Warwick, and lord of Baddesley Clinton. By the time Edward IV came to the throne, however, he had ceased to busy himself with public affairs, and had instead decided to expend all his energies on the advancement of his children.

His daughter Jocosa became Prioress at the Wroxhall Nunnery, and his son Thomas lived in the manor house of Woodloes, close by Warwick, a very substantial property.

But the time came when John Herthill, steward to the Earl of Warwick, wanted the Woodloes property back. It was Herthill who had negotiated the mortgage between the Earl and John Brome, but John Brome was not going to part with it, and refused to vacate.

The matter dragged on somewhat, with Brome refusing to negotiate further, and his son Thomas still in possession.

Despite all Herthill's pleas, and the Earl's anger, John Brome remained adamant. Herthill decided to take matters into his own hands, and when he learned that John Brome was on a visit to London, he decided to follow him there. He discovered that it was John Brome's custom to worship at White Friars church when in the capital, and accordingly Herthill lay in wait for him.

During divine service, he sent a messenger into the church requesting John Brome to step outside where someone wished to speak with him. When Brome received this message, he came hurrying out into the church porch, and when he spied Herthill he became very angry. He refused to surrender Woodloes, and refused to discuss the matter any further.

Herthill, angered in his turn, took a knife from his clothing and with an oath, stabbed John Brome to the heart.

John Brome's eldest son, Nicholas, inherited Baddesley Clinton, and was by all accounts an extremely hot-headed young man. He bitterly resented the slur cast upon his family by the murder of his father and he vowed vengeance upon its perpetrator, John Herthill.

His anger had to smoulder for some three years until chance threw John Herthill in his path. Nicholas Brome watched for Herthill and noted where he went. One fine autumn day in 1471, he lay in wait for the steward as he crossed Longbridge

Field to go towards the village of Barford, on business for his master the Earl.

Longbridge, in those far-off days, was only a mile from the Earl's great castle, but it was a wild and desolate spot, mostly heathland, and the notorious haunt of footpads and thieves.

Herthill, hurrying across it, must have been aware of the dangers, but he was taken completely by surprise when Nicholas Brome leapt upon him. Herthill had little chance, and after a short and bloody encounter, he fell to the ground dead. Nicholas Brome could be satisfied that he had avenged his dead father, and removed the slur on the family's honour.

He was not to get off entirely scot free, though. Within a few months, in March 1472, Brome was brought before the court in Coventry for this murder. The court, however, had some sympathy for the young man, realising that Herthill had murdered first, and Brome was let off with the proviso that he pay for masses to be said at St Mary's church, Warwick, for the souls of both John Brome and his killer, John Herthill. He also had to pay for masses at Baddesley, and he had to pay a small sum in compensation to Elizabeth Herthill for the loss of her husband and breadwinner.

It would be reasonable to suppose that Nicholas Brome, having got off so lightly, would go home and live a blameless life. But this was not the case.

He did go home, true. And as his father before him, he sought to improve the status of the Brome family.

Some few years passed, and then Nicholas Brome's swift temper once again got the better of him. He returned home from a hunting trip, and striding into his home at Baddesley Clinton, he heard noises coming from the 'best parlour'. Flinging open the door, he saw the local parish priest 'chucking' his young wife under the chin. It was obvious that Nicholas's wife and the parish priest had been enjoying each other's company in the absence of the lord and master, but probably it had gone no further than this. Nicholas Brome did not stop to make enquiries, however. He once again raised his fists and set about the poor parish priest, so that the man fell dead at his feet.

Once again Nicholas Brome had murdered! And killing a priest was a far more serious offence than killing a steward!

He made a clean breast of the affair, and petitioned for a pardon from both the King (Henry VII) and the Pope.

He was told that a pardon would be granted to him if he performed some acts of expiation. Accordingly, he built a tower at his own parish church of St James, Baddesley Clinton. He raised the body of the church by some ten feet, and beautified much of the nave. He provided three bells to go within the tower, and then casting about for something more to do, he paid for repairs to the nearby church of Packwood.

The promised pardon was granted to him on completion of all these works, in 1496.

Nicholas Brome died in 1517, and in a final act of humility ordered that his body be buried beneath a stone near to the church door '. . . as people may tread on mee when they come into the Church'. This was carried out in accordance with his wishes, and the spot is marked by a simple slab which reads 'Nicholas Brome 1517'. People do still need to walk across it as they enter the church.

Nicholas Brome is in good company though, for twelve generations of his descendants followed him into the little church, although none of them bore the name Brome. His heir was his daughter, Constantia, who married Sir Edward Ferrers, and so the manor house of Nicholas Brome passed into the Ferrers family.

The Scandalous George Eliot

IN the early hours of the morning on 22nd November 1819, a little girl was born at Arbury Farm, near Nuneaton; a little girl who was ultimately to achieve both fame and notoriety; the first because of her novels, and the second because of her deliberately chosen life style. The first should have earned her a place in Westminster Abbey upon her death, but the second prevented such a place being offered.

Mary Anne Evans was the third child of Christiana and Robert Evans. Robert was the land agent to Mr Francis Parker-Newdigate at Arbury Hall, the beautiful old grey manor house that Mary Anne Evans, as George Eliot, was to take as the pattern for Cheverel Manor in *Scenes of Clerical Life*.

The family moved to Griff House, just outside Nuneaton, when Mary Anne was a few months old, and it was here that the little girl spent her childhood. She went for rides, wandered the lanes and fields, accompanied her father when he went to Arbury Hall and went everywhere she could with her adored older brother Isaac. Their relationship was a very close one, and she drew upon it heavily later when she wrote of Tom and Maggie Tulliver in *The Mill on the Floss*.

Mary Anne loved her home at Griff House, and must have remembered it all very vividly, for she drew upon her memories for all her novels. 'Darlcote Mill' looked very like Griff House.

The gardens appeared again in *Adam Bede* and in *Middlemarch*. Chilvers Coton church close by became 'Shepperton Church' in *Scenes of Clerical Life*. She also based many of the facets of her characters on those people whom she had met in childhood.

Mary Anne and Isaac attended the dame school on the opposite side of the road to Griff House, and later the little girl joined her big sister at boarding school in nearby Attleborough. Mary Anne is described as an awkward and very serious child with a passion for reading.

In 1841 Isaac married and Robert Evans, now widowed for the second time, decided to retire, leaving Isaac to carry on as land agent and to live with his bride at Griff House. Robert and his daughter, Mary Anne, moved to Bird Grove, a fairly large house on the outskirts of Coventry. They were both active members of Holy Trinity in Coventry.

It was here at Bird Grove that Mary Anne met neighbours who were to have a profound influence on her. Charles Bray was a ribbon manufacturer, who lived with his wife Cara. He was also a philosopher and free thinker, and around him he gathered those of like persuasion. The conversation was brilliant and witty, and Mary Anne couldn't get enough of it.

Charles Bray had long divested himself of the religion in which he had been brought up, and talking to Mary Anne, she too began to have strong doubts. She refused to accompany her father to church and this so distressed him that he sent Mary Anne back to Isaac and his wife for a while, and threatened to sell Bird Grove and go to live with his other children elsewhere.

Mary Anne relented, returned home and once more went with her father to church, although in reality she had become an agnostic.

In 1848 Robert Evans died, and Mary Anne was devastated by his death. The Brays took her with them on holiday, thinking this would help her to get over her bereavement. Mary Anne had already tried her hand at writing, some of which had been published in the *Coventry Herald*, owned by Mr

Bray. Her father's death left her with a little money and accordingly when she returned from her holiday in Geneva, she changed her name to the more fashionable Marian and went to London, where she rapidly fell in with John Chapman, of the *Westminster Review*.

She went to live with him and his wife, and he declared he needed her both to write and to help him edit. His wife, however, became hostile towards Marian, believing that she and John Champman were conducting an affair.

It was at the Chapman house, where many of the literati were wont to congregate, that Marian met George Lewes, another writer, but whose writings have remained somewhat obscure. He was described as 'small and pockmarked' and 'the ugliest man in London'. Marian was also described by some as ugly, but she must have had some attractions, for she collected many men around her, often to the discomfiture of their wives.

Lewes was already married; his wife believed in what is now called an 'open marriage' and had borne children to George's best friend. In order to protect the children, Lewes had allowed the infants to be registered in his name and had thus, in the eyes of the law, condoned his wife's adultery. Divorce was, therefore, out of the question.

Marian and George Lewes began to live together as man and wife and in July 1854, they went abroad quite openly together. This terrible scandal caused her beloved brother Isaac to refuse to speak to her and cut her off from many old friends in her native heath.

It was Lewes who created George Eliot. He persuaded Marian to try her hand at fiction, and she produced *The Sad Fortunes of the Rev Amos Barton* which he sent off to Blackwoods as being from a 'clerical friend'. Marian received 50 guineas for it, and from that time on her true career began. She chose the pen name 'George Eliot' with Lewes's help. George was his name, and Marian rather liked 'Eliot' because it was a good round mouthful!

Marian lived with Lewes as his wife for 24 years. She

became devoted to his son, Charles, and nursed his other son in his last illness. She and Lewes helped and encouraged each other's literary efforts and Lewes in effect acted as her manager. They led a happy and interesting life and as the novels of George Eliot were eagerly received, they became prosperous enough to enjoy a comfortable lifestyle.

Then George Lewes died in November 1878 and Marian was utterly devastated, so much so that she refused to see anybody other than his son, Charles. In 1879, she was persuaded to complete *Impressions of Theophrastus Such* but it was not as well received as her other works.

One of the greatest friends of both Marian and the late George Lewes was Johnnie Cross, and he persuaded her to face the world again and take up other interests. He then proposed to her, not once, but several times, and she was eventually to agree, although he was only 40, good looking and eligible, and she was by this time 60 and in poor health.

They were married on 6th May 1880, and immediately set off for a honeymoon in Venice. It was at this time that a strange incident occurred which has never been properly explained, at least not publicly. On the second day of his honeymoon Johnnie Cross jumped from the balcony of the hotel into the Grand Canal. It was put down to 'temporary mental derangement', but others called it 'attempted suicide'. Whatever the reason for this extraordinary behaviour, he recovered, and the couple returned to England to their new house in Cheyne Walk.

On 22nd December, only a few months later, George Eliot died, and Johnnie Cross was with her at the end. Her marriage to him had at last healed the breach between herself and her brother Isaac and her friends in Nuneaton. Isaac was stern and unbending, and living in sin was not acceptable in rural Warwickshire circles.

Johnnie Cross urged that George Eliot should be buried in Westminster Abbey – the extent, the volume and the quality of her work merited it. But after her many years of unconventional living with George Lewes, and her refusal to accept

Church teachings, the Dean of Westminster refused to allow it.

She was buried in unconsecrated ground at Highgate Cemetery, next to the grave of George Lewes. Johnnie Cross mourned her and visited the childhood haunts in Warwickshire which she had written about so lovingly. He never married again and died in 1924.

George Eliot's novels, widely acclaimed almost from the start, continue to arouse great interest, as does their author's life. Many visitors arrive in Nuneaton and Chilvers Coton every year on the 'George Eliot Trail'. A George Eliot Memorial Garden was founded in 1951, and each autumn a dinner is held in her honour, as close as possible to her birthday.

George Eliot eventually received recognition from her native Warwickshire, but it was a long time coming!

The
Haunted
Battlefield

A T Edgehill field, in the Vale of the Red Horse, on that fateful day of 23rd October 1642, the opposing armies of King Charles I and Parliament met headlong in the first battle of the English Civil War. Many tales and legends have arisen from this bloody and terrible event, for war between neighbour and neighbour, brother and brother, is surely the most dreadful war of all.

The King and his Royalists were marching from Shrewsbury towards Banbury, when Lord Essex with the Parliamentary troops decided to intercept them, to protect the Banbury garrison.

They came together and faced each other at Edgehill. Up until this time, it had been vainly thought that the war might not happen, that both sides would see reason, but after Edgehill, there was no doubt at all that the country was plunged into civil war.

The King and his troops were at the top of the Edgehill escarpment, when Essex and his troops rode out from the nearby small town of Kineton to meet them. The battle raged around Edgehill plain for the whole day, and many valiant and daring deeds were witnessed on both sides. Captain John Smith, brother to Lord Carrington, and a most brave gentleman, rode right into the ranks of the Roundhead army to recapture the King's standard so that the Royalists would not know it had been captured and thus lose heart. He was knighted by the King as he rode back with it.

When the day was over, night fell, bitterly cold. To neither side had gone a clear-cut victory, but Prince Rupert's men had ridden into Kineton and sacked it. The dead and wounded lay upon the battlefield all night, and as dawn broke were attended by two surgeons, one of whom was William Harvey, to whose work we owe our present knowledge about the circulation of the blood.

Reports on the numbers of dead vary enormously, some putting it at about 1,500 and others as high as 6,000. Many of the wounded were saved by the coldness of the night which prevented them from bleeding to death.

It was round about Christmas time, two months later, that the strange happenings began. Just about two weeks before the Yuletide festival, several shepherds, 'poor, ignorant men', rushed into Kineton and reported that for three hours they had watched terrified as the great battle had been re-enacted in the sky.

On the bloodstained grass of the field, they had stood, transfixed with fear, as they listened to the sound of clashing sabres and muffled drum beats. They heard horses pounding across the torn turf, and the shrieks and groans of wounded and dying men. They heard martial cries, the sound of the cornet, shouts of command, the crack of the musket and the boom of cannon. The sky had been filled with a great light, they said, and only when it all died down had they been able to move again, to run back to their home at Kineton, and tell the story.

The vicar of Kineton, Mr Samuel Marshall, and Mr William Wood, a JP, heard the shepherds' tale with scepticism. Despite intensive questioning, the shepherds stuck to their story, and on the following night they returned to Edgehill, accompanied by Mr Marshall and Mr Wood. Once again, the same ghostly re-enactment occurred.

On the Saturday of the following week, many reliable and

respectable witnesses saw the same ghostly happening, and the whole area was in a state of turmoil and tumult. People were afraid to go out of their houses, pregnant women miscarried, and everyone was too terrified to do anything.

The King, then at Oxford, was informed, and he sent six especially selected officers of unimpeachable integrity to visit Kineton, and report back to him. They were taken to the scene, and they too witnessed the great tumult in the sky. They saw their dead comrades in the thick of the fray; they heard their own command, and they saw the entire battle as they, who had been present, had seen it on the day of 23rd October. Visibly shaken, they returned to Oxford to tell the King.

Some learned men, hearing of this phenomenon, suggested that some bodies of the slain might still remain on the battlefield, undiscovered, beneath scrub and furze, and accordingly a search was carried out. Several such bodies were found and given Christian burial, and the inhabitants of Kineton hoped this might be the end of their troublous visitation, but it was not to be.

In January, a London printer called Thomas Jackson, issued a pamphlet called *The New Yeare's Wonder* giving full and authenticated details of the sightings.

And now more than three centuries later, the battlefield is still haunted. The land where once the great battle raged is now in the hands of the Army authorities, and it is not possible to venture across it. Yet visitations have been seen intermittently from time to time, and there are other lonely spectres on this ghostly field.

There is a white horse that wanders across the Edgehill plain looking for its slain master, the Royalist Kingsmill, who is buried nearby in the village of Radway. A worn effigy can be seen in the little church there, erected by his family after the end of the Civil War. A posy often appears on Kingsmill's tomb, but no one ever admits to having put it there.

There is also the tale of the bloodstained barn where a Royalist officer sheltered, and the blood from his many wounds ran down from the upper storey. This too manifests itself, and then disappears.

Local land names bear witness to the battle. Graveground Coppice, where many of the dead were buried in a mass grave, and where local dogs refuse to venture. The Red Road, a mere bridlepath now, but so-called because it once ran red with blood.

A marker stone on the road from Kineton, nearest to the battle site, commemorates the bloody affray.

The
Killing of
Constable Hine

THE murder of young Police Constable William Hine at
Fenny Compton, a small village set amid the Dassett
Hills in the south of the county, is one of our most famous, or
perhaps infamous unsolved crimes. Constable Hine was killed
while on duty, and his name is thus on the police Roll of
Honour.

It was a dark Monday evening, 15th February 1886, when
30 year old William Hine, big, broad-shouldered, fit and
athletic, left his home in the village for his customary night
patrol. Being the village constable, Hine walked all around his
patch every night, calling finally at the village inn, the George
and Dragon, where he exchanged a pleasant word or two with
the landlord and the customers, and remained to see the inn
properly cleared at closing time. William Hine, who had been
in the force less than two years, was a bit of a stickler for the
letter of the law.

On this fateful night, he said 'Goodnight' to the landlord,
and that was the last time anybody in Fenny Compton saw
William Hine alive. He did not return to his home and by the
early hours of the morning his young wife, having received no
word from him, became alarmed. She reported that he had
not returned home and a search was immediately under way.

His helmet was found in a field just outside the village.

There were also signs of a struggle, the grass in the field being a bit churned up, but what was more significant was the fact that the grass bore unmistakable traces of blood. Whose blood? Constable Hine's pocket handkerchief, identified by his wife, and also bearing bloodstains was found beneath the hedge, but of the man himself there was no sign.

The search continued. Locals were closely questioned, and Mrs Hine was frantic with worry, but since the constable had left the village inn, nobody had seen him anywhere.

Three days later, a knife belonging to William Hine was found hidden, buried deep inside a bramble bush.

In response to questioning, one or two locals came forward and told of hearing a pony and trap go through the village on the night the constable disappeared. The reason it was noticed at all was because it was well past midnight, and in a sleepy little village like Fenny Compton, it was a most unusual occurrence. Having been awakened, and peering through their windows, the villagers believed that there were four men in the trap, which went through at a fair pace.

They were certainly not locals, the police were assured. After all, nobody up to any good drives horse-drawn vehicles at that time of night, and certainly nobody living in the village would do so. Valiant attempts were made to trace the four strangers, but with no success.

It was not until the eighth day after his disappearance that the body of William Hine was discovered in the canal, half a mile from the old wharf at Fenny Compton. A post-mortem revealed he had died from a knife wound in his neck which had pierced the jugular vein.

It was obvious that robbery was not the motive for this crime; or at least not the robbery of the constable, for he still had his watch in his pocket and his money, not a large amount, was found still intact in his sodden uniform.

Enquiries intensified and a substantial reward was offered for any information that might help police track down the murderer or murderers. In 1886, the sum of £250 was a lot of money, but even this did not bring forth fruit. No one came forward, either because no one knew any more than they had already told, or because they knew too much and were frightened.

The killing of Constable William Hine, who was abroad in the course of his public duty, remains unsolved. It may have been that he surprised the four men while they were engaged on some nefarious business, and they overpowered him, dragged him into the field, and silenced him forever. Athletic and strong though he was, he would not have been a match for four desperate ruffians.

No robberies or crimes were reported in that area that night, so if he did surprise the men, they were not able to carry out whatever it was they planned. Perhaps they decided that murder was enough.

Murder
at
Little Kineton

LITTLE Kineton is about a mile from the small market 'town' of Kineton itself. It is a picture-book hamlet, with a wide village green, a pond where ducks skitter among the reeds, benevolent old trees, cottages of mellow stone, and an ancient Victorian letter box treasured by the local inhabitants.

The old manor house among the fields was once the home of the Bentley family, and remained with them for more than two centuries, until a fearful crime caused such havoc within what remained of that family that it virtually died out.

The Bentleys were a well-loved and fairly rollicking family by all accounts. Sir Charles was Sheriff of Warwickshire in 1667 and is described as being 'very rich and very fat'. He was succeeded by his son, another Charles who, mindful of his position, took pains to marry an heiress. However, the bride's family did not think much of the match, and as a consequence became a bit mean about the lady's dowry. The constant battle between her husband and her family over this matter, with the poor bride as 'pig-in-the-middle', upset her and thoroughly soured her disposition, so that the Bentleys were not so rollicking, but were still rich.

The son of this union was a totally different character to those jolly country squires who were his forbears. Edward Bentley was somewhat profligate, preferring the fashionable and expensive life in London where he could spend night after night at the gaming tables. Not for him the life of a country squire, the simple joys of the estate, and the tenants' problems.

He never married, and upon his death all his property was left to his three sisters, Charlotte, Grace and Anne.

As a separate and personal bequest, he left a quantity of handsome plate to Miss Grace, for she had become engaged to young Mr Nicholas, the local curate, and they were soon to be married.

One Sunday morning, in the 1740s, the three pious ladies were at church. The family cook was in the kitchens of the manor house preparing the meal which they would eat later that day, and was accompanied by little five year old Miss Beatrice, the young sister of the amiable curate, Mr Nicholas. Little Beatrice had grown very fond of Miss Grace, who was so soon to become her sister-in-law, and was a frequent visitor to the old house. She loved to play in the gardens, and doubtless she also liked to pester the cook for sweetmeats and raisins.

Considered a little too young for morning service, the child had been left in the charge of the cook until the three ladies of the house, and the curate, returned from their devotions.

The rascal in the story was the family coachman, not long in their employment. This morning he decided the coast was clear enough to put into operation a plan of action he had long entertained, to steal the pieces of plate belonging to Miss Grace. The cook was busy in her kitchen. The family were at church for at least another hour. The opportunity was too good to miss, he decided.

However, he had reckoned without the acute hearing of the cook, who heard noises from the dining room and came in to investigate. There she spotted the villain just loading the pieces of plate into a large sack. She slammed the door and rushed back into the kitchen, but the coachman, knowing he had been discovered, followed her. Grabbing a meat cleaver from the scrubbed wooden table, he used it to silence the screaming cook, and clove her head clean in two. Following the first blow with many others, he at last threw down the bloody weapon and took to his heels.

The family returned from their prayers to a scene of carnage. But where was little Miss Beatrice? Search as they might, they could not find the child, and were fearful that she too might have met a bloody end, or even that the murderer might have taken her with him.

Beatrice, however, seems to have been possessed of more sense than her elders gave her credit for, and she was eventually discovered hiding inside the old fire copper in the corner of the kitchen. What's more, she was playing quite happily with a set of playing cards. She had witnessed the murder and had crept softly away before the coachman, in his act of desperate madness, had even known she was present.

The coachman did not get very far, was relatively easily apprehended and was ultimately hanged for his crime.

The little girl was made much of, and in fact had her portrait painted holding in her hand the self-same playing cards that had kept her occupied within the old brick copper. This portrait hung for a long time in a private collection in a house at Burton Dassett, about ten miles from Kineton, but alas its present whereabouts are unknown.

Sadly Miss Grace never did get to marry Mr Nicholas. The horror of this Sunday morning, and the sight which had met her eyes on her return to the house, all had a dreadful effect upon her. She became ill and died shortly afterwards. She lies buried in the old churchyard at Kineton. Two years later, little Beatrice died too, and she was buried near to her very 'dear Miss Grace'. The heartbroken Mr Nicholas left the area.

The other two sisters, Miss Charlotte and Miss Anne, continued to live on in the old house until their deaths, when the property passed out of the hands of the Bentley family.

The
Mystery of
Salford Hall

IN the tragic aftermath of the French Revolution, a group of nuns of the English Benedictine order fled from Cambrai, where they had been an established community since 1625, and came to live in Salford Hall, in the lush fruit-growing valley of the Avon, in south-west Warwickshire. In 1808 they opened a convent and boarding school for young ladies.

The mystery of Salford Hall began on 15th June 1815 when a middle-aged American gentleman asked to speak to the Abbess, Dame Burgoyne, and handed over to her two more pupils, girls aged about 11 and 13. He also handed over to her an envelope containing explicit instructions, and a large sum of money.

He explained to her that he was not of her faith, nor as far as he knew were the girls. He had been in France during the most fearful scenes of the Revolution, and had been impressed with the courage and fortitude of the Benedictine sisters. When he heard they had found a safe home in England, and 'as dangers were thickening round me and mine' he resolved to entrust his wards to their care. He said his name was Herbert Dingwall.

Herbert Dingwall then left as unceremoniously as he had arrived, not even stopping to bid farewell to the children.

The little girls told Dame Burgoyne their names were

Wyom and Evra Hendon, and as far as they knew their Papa had run a silver mine in Nevada in partnership with Herbert Dingwall. Beyond this they seemed to know very little.

The Abbess was mystified. When she opened the packet Dingwall had handed over to her she found that there was sufficient money to pay for the girls' schooling, plus clothing, extras, vacation expenses and pocket money.

The accompanying letter explained that when Wyom, the elder of the two, had been at Salford Hall for five years, the Abbess was to insert an advertisement in the *Times* newspaper for nine days running. They were to be guided by the terms of any reply that came in answer to the advertisement. Should no reply be forthcoming, then the girls were to be told they were penniless orphans, and must make shift for their own living as best they might.

The little girls seemed perfectly content to settle down at Salford Hall, and prattled away in answer to the good Dame's questions. They had, it seems, lived in many places, and had been to many schools, until their father sent them home to England where they had lived with Herbert Dingwall in Liverpool. But then Herbert had changed, had seemed to get worried and frightened, and had brought them here.

The five years quickly passed; the girls were able scholars. Wyom grew tall and graceful, was well-read and full of life and humour. Evra was shorter, more rounded, and of a much more dreamy and and introspective disposition. They were utterly devoted to each other, and together they became popular among both the nuns and the other pupils. However, at times, the Abbess fancied they appeared 'set apart' and she was convinced they knew more of their background than they had told her.

The time grew near to insert the curiously-worded advertisement. The girls' schooling was almost at an end, and now Wyom chose to confide in the Abbess. She said she had last seen her father in Boston (USA) when he had told her he came of an English family of noble birth, and although he was the scapegrace, having run off to seek his fortune, nevertheless the estate was entailed and he would inherit it. Wyom and Evra were, therefore, heiresses. It seems that Hendon believed Dingwall to be a man of integrity, but had grave doubts about Dingwall's son, and had made Wyom solemnly promise that no matter what happened, she would never agree to marriage with this young man.

On 15th June 1820 the advertisement duly appeared in the *Times*. On the ninth day a letter came from London, curt and to the point, instructing the Abbess that Wyom Hendon was to go to Holt House, Graybourne, Buckingham. She was to start out the following week, taking the coach from Stratford-on-Avon, and in Buckingham she would be met and escorted to her new home.

The sisters, who had never before been separated, were inconsolable, but at last amid tearful farewells, Wyom set forth on her journey. She promised to write within the week, but no letter came. Evra pined, and refused to eat. The Abbess grew daily more worried, but still no news of Wyom. Dame Burgoyne herself wrote to the Buckingham address, but there was no reply.

Weeks passed; the school broke up for holidays, and then reassembled. Among the pupils was Miss Alice Payton, who had chosen to return for an extra year to pursue special studies. Her father delivered her to Salford Hall and paused for a word with Dame Burgoyne, asking for news of Wyom.

'No news', the Abbess sadly replied. 'We have heard no word of her, although I have myself written twice to the Graybourne address.'

'But Reverend Mother', cried Alice, 'there is no such place in Buckinghamshire.' And her father readily confirmed this. 'I have lived in Buckinghamshire, and have followed the hounds over every inch of that county', he declared. 'There is no such place. . .'

Mr Payton, a magistrate, shared the Abbess's fears for the fate of Wyom. They warned Alice to say nothing to Evra for fear this would cause the girl to go into the decline which already threatened. Mr Payton promised to make enquiries, and this he faithfully did, but to no avail. It seems that Wyom had vanished. He wrote to tell the Abbess of his failure in this direction, and in reply she wrote to him to tell him of the curious sleep-walking habits that Evra had recently developed.

Several times the nuns had discovered Evra's bed empty and had searched the house, fearing for her safety. When they returned to the dormitory, it was to find Evra sleeping peacefully in her bed.

The girl was becoming completely distraught. The nuns did not speak to her about sleep-walking, but one of them kept watch each night. Eventually Evra confided in Dame Burgoyne, saying she constantly heard Wyom's voice calling to her, and she had to leave her bed to go to her sister. She always found herself in a passage with a window at the end. The blind was drawn down over the window, and she could not see through into the room beyond, but she knew Wyom was there. She heard her weeping and she heard two men threatening Wyom, trying to get the girl to sign a legal paper, which she refused to do.

Evra continued to experience these visions with increasing intensity, and still there was no word of Wyom. Ultimately, poor Evra spent more time in the 'other' world of her visions than in this one and fell into a melancholy madness, with the good sisters caring for her lovingly.

Wyom had been gone for many months, when once more Evra rose from her bed. Thin, emaciated, frail and pale with hollow, haunted eyes, Evra once more followed Wyom's voice, and the nuns heard her cry 'O my poor sister! You shall not kill her! You are not my sister's husband; your name is not "Allen" but Dingwall. . . .' Then with a last piercing shriek, Evra cried aloud 'O Wyom! O Wyom! He has killed me, and I came only to save you. . . .'

When the nuns eventually found Evra she was lying peacefully in her own bed; but poor Evra was dead.

Some months later, Mr Payton, Alice's father, was performing his duties as a magistrate when a man was brought before him charged with attempting to murder his wife. The story that unfolded was not a pretty one.

It seems that the man, 'Allen', lived in an isolated house, with one other man and an old woman as their servant. They had fairly recently been joined by a young lady, whom Allen referred to as his wife. The household had been the subject of much local gossip. Screams were heard at night and trades-men were not welcomed, their goods snatched from their hands with the door opened but a crack. Whenever the young lady had shown her face beyond the door, she had been pulled back indoors by rough hands.

One night a doctor was called in to the young lady, who it was said, had 'fallen down the stairs'. The doctor realised this could not be true after he had seen her injuries. Upon his second visit, the man 'Allen' said to him 'Don't you think my wife exhibits all the signs of insanity?' The doctor replied that he saw no such signs, whereupon he was rudely told to go away and not return.

Several months later, another doctor was called in to attend the same young woman, who was suffering from stab wounds. This doctor realised the danger the young woman was in. 'Allen' danced about like a madman and had a knife in his hand, with which he threatened the doctor more than once. But what was really driving 'Allen' crazy he said was the ghost of an unnamed girl who every night came in through the window, and wouldn't leave him alone. 'That girl comes between me and my wife', he yelled. 'I will give her more . . . I will give her more. . . .' and he frothed at the mouth.

The doctor managed to overcome the near-crazed man and have him taken in charge, while he turned his full attention to the young woman, who was in a critical condition.

As soon as the man 'Allen' and his story came before Mr Payton, the magistrate knew at once that this man was Dingwall junior, and that the young woman was Wyom.

In court, Dingwall swore it was his partner Grant who had put him up to the whole thing, but on the night of the stabbing, Grant had run off, and was never seen again. Dingwall was in due course sentenced to transportation.

Wyom eventually recovered, and told her story. She said the men had tried to make her either marry 'Allen' or sign a legal document making over her inheritance to him, and she had consistently refused to do either. In her most fearful moments she had called upon her sister Evra, who had appeared on the other side of the window of the room. Both men had seen her and become terrified; so terrified that on occasions they had both run from the room.

Wyom was told of her sister's death and its circumstances when she was sufficiently recovered, and she visited Evra's grave and heard the whole story from the nuns at Salford Hall.

There is a happy outcome! Wyom eventually married the doctor who had saved her, and some eleven years or so later the sisters at Salford Hall had another pupil, little Miss Wyom Evra Hendon Lepel.

Mr Payton, intrigued by the whole thing, busied himself measuring all the walls at Salford Hall, and he did discover to his own satisfaction that if the passageway described by Evra had indeed existed where she said it was, by the side of the chapel, and if it had been extended in a perfectly straight line, it would have gone straight through the middle of the isolated house in Buckingham!

Disaster
at
Baddesley Mine

BAXTERLEY, a small village in the mining area of north Warwickshire, has never forgotten a fine spring day in 1882, more than a century ago. There is a brass plate on the wall of the little church to remind them that on 2nd May 1882, the worst colliery disaster in the history of the Warwickshire coalfield happened at nearby Baddesley Mine.

It was pit deputy Charles Day and his son Joseph, a collier, who gave the alarm. They had been carrying out a perfectly normal routine inspection during the night of the 2nd May, when they were quite suddenly met with dense and suffocating smoke in the up-cast shaft of the Stratford Pit. They then found that the down-cast shaft was also filled with smoke to within a few inches of the floor, where signs of fresh air remained.

The Days were well aware that nine men were working beyond the wall of smoke, deep within the bowels of the mine. Immediately, they sent for the manager, and joined by 36 of their colleagues, they concentrated their efforts on diverting the smoke. The pit was owned by Mr William Stratford Dugdale, who lived at nearby Merevale Hall. As soon as the news reached him, and he saw the heavy pall of smoke encircling the village, he rushed to join his men in their rescue attempts.

A boiler had recently been installed at the foot of the up-cast shaft to remove water from the deep workings, and the engine was later judged to have been improperly positioned and lacking protection. It was also found that the pit deputies had not followed printed instructions. 'Had they done so', said the Coroner when an inquest was eventually held, 'the true condition of the Pit would have been revealed and loss of life therefore avoided. . . .'

It transpired that many of the men working down the pit were aware of the dangers concerning this engine, which had apparently never worked properly.

The engine was accommodated in the deep return airway by widening the shaft and removing the ceiling. In addition to exposing the funnel to the highly inflammable layer of coal immediately above, excavated coal was piled close by. So close, in fact, that it came into contact with burning ashes from the faulty engine.

Even on the night before the tragedy, there had been a small fire which had been quickly dowsed by the night men.

When the dense smoke was discovered in the up-cast shaft, it was also found that a door had been opened, and this had allowed the smoke to penetrate into the deep, the most immediate threat to the men working down there.

All through that fateful night men worked tirelessly, struggling against overwhelming odds to reach their nine fellow colliers. Beaten back time and time again by continuing explosions, injured by collapsing debris, burned by the flames roaring out at them and suffocated by gases, nevertheless the work went on. Men were dragged from the pit in a state of collapse, and their place was immediately taken by others.

The work continued throughout the next day, until it became all too obvious that rescue was impossible. The nine, eight men and a boy, trapped a mile below the surface with eleven pit ponies, could not be reached. It was also realised with full horror that even if they could reach them, they must by this time have perished, suffocated by the smoke and gas.

The fire spread until the pit was an inferno. Poisonous fumes poured out and the smoke could be seen for miles. A decision was taken to seal off the mine and thus extinguish the flames, but this too was found almost impossible. Below the ground it was like a volcano, and the rush of fire and gas blew the seals away with explosion after explosion.

By the time the mine was finally sealed off, another twelve men had died as well as the first nine victims.

The courage of the rescuers was astounding, and almost all of them had sustained severe injuries. Some were dragged out only to die within minutes, others died days later. One by one the death toll mounted.

Mr Dugdale, the owner, had struggled all night alongside his men. At one stage he disappeared completely underground, and it was only when two colliers heard his cries, that he was found desperately injured. It was with the greatest difficulty they got him to the surface.

He spent many days in agony. Not only was he in great physical pain, but the responsibility of owning a mine in which so many lives had been lost played heavily on his mind. He could not forget his men who died.

Almost his last words were 'Have I the people's good will . . . ?' On being reassured that the people thought well of him, as they had always done, he said 'Then I shall die happy, for I am dying with my people . . .'

Charles Day, the Pit Deputy, was among the most valiant in his rescue attempts, and on that awful night he lost three brave sons.

The nine who perished were William Blower, 26; William Knight, 31; Joseph Orton, 35; George Bates, 38; William Smith, 46; John Ross, 51; Henry Radford, 51; and William Day, 71. Plus young Joseph Scattergood, aged just 13 years old. Not a home in the area remained untouched by the tragedy, and despite immense courage on the part of the rescuers, the final death toll was 32.

Those who survived never forgot the ordeal of that night, and it was a very long time before the village of Baxterley, and other villages round about, emerged from their mourning.

The Wroth Silver Ceremony

THE origins of this curious and peculiarly Warwickshire custom are lost in the mists of antiquity. It is one of the few local customs that has survived unscathed; its form slightly altered, but in essence the same.

The ceremony takes place at Knightlow Cross, on Knightlow Hill, an ancient tumulus not far from Dunchurch, in the old Hundred of Knightlow, on St Martin's Day (11th November) just as the sun rises.

The tumulus is about 30 ft round at the top, and upon it is what remains of an old 14th century preaching cross, a large square stone, with a hollow in the middle where once the shaft of the cross rose. The stone still carries the mason's marks.

In the hollow of this stone, the 'silver' is collected. Representatives from all the parishes within the Hundred of Knightlow, gather to pay their 'Wroth' to the Lord of the Hundred, the Duke of Buccleuch.

The Duke's Steward reads out to the crowd the Charter of Assembly. One by one the parishes are called, throwing the coins into the hollow stone and saying the words 'Wroth Silver'. Failure to pay the dues results in a fine, or the forfeit of a wild white bull with a red nose and ears of the same colour.

In Anglo-Saxon the word 'weorth' meant prize money, and it is thought this money was originally paid over to the lord for

101

his protection. Not only protection of person, but protection of possessions such as cattle and pigs, for once upon a time this was a wild and barren heath, with all the consequent terrors, so that taking beasts across it was a hazardous business.

The first mention of the Hundred of Knightlow was in 1170, and it remained with the Crown until 1629 when King Charles I granted it to Sir Francis Leigh. Through him it descended to the Dukes of Buccleuch and Queensbury, with whom it still remains.

There have been some slight changes over the years. Nowadays, not all Hundred parishes are called, nor do they send a representative. The halfpenny 'due' once meant something, but the few pence exacted nowadays is really more of a token than anything else.

A notice of the ceremony appears in the local paper a couple of weeks before the 11th November, for despite the early hour a large crowd usually gathers to watch. The local hostelry, the Old Bull and Butcher, opens up early.

As the first fingers of sunrise light up the sky, and as soon as it is reasonably possible to read it, the Steward reads the Charter and the ceremony begins. It takes but a few minutes, and then all those present retire to the Old Bull and Butcher for a hearty and ceremonial breakfast. At one time the breakfast used to be at the Duke's expense, but now tickets are sold for it, and are usually sold out well in advance! The breakfast is rounded off with a mug of hot milk laced with rum and this is used for the traditional toast to the 'Duke of Buccleuch'.

No one has for years been required to pay the forfeit, although it did happen once in the 19th century. However, the beast when it was received, was rejected out of hand because neither its ears nor its nose were red, nor was it particularly wild!

It is believed that wild white cattle used to roam this heath, and it was probably one of these that gave rise to the legend of Guy of Warwick and the Dun Cow.

The collection of monies for the protection of cattle did once take place elsewhere in the country. It was usually called by another name, often 'Rother' money, since 'rother' means cattle, and in some towns 'Rother Street' was once the site of the cattle market. Most of these ceremonies have come to an end, though. Fortunately, the one in Warwickshire continues unabated, with more people watching it every year.

The Lady of Barrells

L ITTLE now remains of the grandeur that was once Barrells Hall, between Henley-in-Arden and Ullenhall, just to the north of Stratford-on-Avon. The beautiful gardens that so delighted the heart of the Lady Luxborough and her friends are gone. The house was severely damaged by a fire in 1933, since which time its sightless eyes have gazed across a dank wilderness, and it has remained unihabited, except for the pale ghost on the great staircase.

It was the Knight family from nearby Worcestershire who first acquired the land at Barrells in 1554. They were yeoman farmers, but not for long. After they moved over the border into Warwickshire, their ascent up the social ladder went at quite a pace. Their old farmhouse gradually grew and came to be called the manor house, and when William Knight died in 1651, he was succeeded by his son, John. His second son, Robert, decided to leave his brother in charge at Barrells, while he went off to seek his fortune in the City.

He seems to have made slow progress, but his son, also Robert (2nd) became involved in the now notorious South Sea Company. This extraordinary undertaking caused a tidal wave of speculation in the famed fabulous wealth of the South Seas. Eventually the bubble burst in scandal with allegations of financial fraud on all sides. Robert Knight fled to France.

He was pardoned in 1742 and returned home to England, but died two years later leaving the enormous fortune he had gained through the South Sea Bubble to his son, Robert (3rd).

This Robert married Henrietta, daughter of Sir Henry St John. Three years after their marriage, Robert bought the estate at Barrells from his cousin, Raleigh Knight, doubtless using some of the South Sea Bubble plunder.

The marriage of Robert and Henrietta was not a happy one, although two sons and a daughter were born to them. Robert Knight cast about for a way of ridding himself of his wife, and upon discovering that a friendship existed between Henrietta and a clergyman, tutor of the son of a friend, he chose to read into this all the signs of infidelity. His own life was far from blameless, and Henrietta's friendship in what must have been a lonely life, appears to have been quite innocent, but her husband chose to think otherwise.

Henrietta was banished to Barrells in 1736, with an allowance of £500 a year, and more than seven servants. She was never to venture more than twenty miles, although twice in her lifetime she was given permission to visit Bath and take the waters for her health.

Henrietta's greatest sorrow was in not being allowed to see her children, and some of her letters reveal just how lonely she was.

Robert Knight was elevated to the peerage in 1745 as Baron Luxborough, and thus Henrietta became Lady Luxborough.

Realising she was powerless against her husband, Henrietta settled down to make the best of her life at Barrells. The current fashion was for landscape gardening, and in this she revelled, creating 'vistas', planting 'avenues', making a 'ravine' and a 'ha-ha', and scattering urns all over the place!

She gathered around her many men of letters, and was a great encouragement to the budding Richard Jago. Perhaps her best friend was the poet William Shenstone (of Halesowen) to whom she wrote long and often. She and Mr Shenstone appear to have vied with each other in the creation of landscapes. Henrietta wrote describing how she was making a coppice to turn towards the Bank, where she proposed to have a seat above the 'the pit'.

Lady Luxborough became one of the most colourful personages in Warwickshire in the 18th century. Beautiful, vivacious, a lively and prolific correspondent, a patron of the arts, and a leader of what eventually became known as the Warwickshire 'Coterie'. Yet she lived a virtual prisoner at Barrells Hall, her heart saddened by her enforced separation from her children.

Lady Luxborough died in 1756 at the age of 57, after 20 years in exile, and was buried in the church at Wootton Wawen.

In 1761, Robert Knight was given further honours, and was created Viscount Barrells and Earl of Catherlough. Shortly after this he decided to practically rebuild Barrells and to create a magnificent mausoleum in Henrietta's garden. he had all his family's coffins removed from Wootton Wawen, all in one go, and reinterred in this mausoleum.

By 1830, the mausoleum had fallen into decay, and all the coffins were once again disturbed, removed, and reinterred in the old church at Ullenhall, where two tablets in the chancel summarise the rise and the fall of the Knights of Barrells.

The ghost of poor sad Lady Luxborough haunts the home she was once forced to occupy in loneliness. The great staircase, or most of it, remains, and upon it may sometimes be seen her slim and shadowy figure, her black hair in elaborate curls, her dress of palest blue silk with lace at her elbows, and upon her face a smile of great sadness. Her spectre is not a fearful one, and has been seen upon many occasions. Perhaps she laments the loss of her urns, vistas and ravines, for these all disappeared long, long ago.

The Abduction of Jane Puckering

LITTLE now remains of Warwick Priory which used to stand near the centre of our county town. In its parkland Warwick people strolled happily, in its pools they fished, but now more or less the only reminder is the name 'Priory Park'.

The grand old house which was built on the site of the old priory in 1566 seems to have brought none of its owners any luck at all! Particularly unfortunate was the young heiress, Jane Puckering.

Serjeant Puckering, Keeper of the Great Seal, came into possession of the house in the late 1500s. Serjeant Puckering's only 'claim to fame' was that he recommended that the sentence of death against Mary, Queen of Scots, should be carried out. He was knighted in 1594 and died the following year, leaving a son, Thomas, as his heir to the Priory.

Thomas Puckering was a man of experience and education. He had travelled much, and learned from all he saw. A man of refinement and sensitivity, he was for several years the representative of Warwick in Parliament.

Alas, the illustrious Thomas died all too soon, leaving only one child, a daughter, Jane Puckering, who was weak and sickly. She was now an heiress, for to her Thomas Puckering left all his wealth and fortune.

Poor Jane seems to have had a most unfortunate life,

through no fault of her own, and throughout the whole of this story she is moved as a chess piece upon a board.

When Jane was about ten years old, the widow, Lady Puckering, petitioned the House of Lords on her behalf. It seems the good lady was anxious because the executors of her late husband's will had got their hands upon large sums of his money, and had taken away little Jane and lodged her with Sir David Cunningham, a complete stranger. By the merest chance (of course) Sir David happened to be related to one of the executors – the very one it seems who was due for an inheritance 'should the child fail'.

The little girl was ailing and lame. She needed her mother, and to be suddenly whisked away and deposited with strangers was causing both mother and child great distress.

Fortunately in this instance the Lords listened to the Lady, and little Jane was restored to her home, with a few more years of peace before she was again pounced upon by those who wished her ill.

In 1649, when Jane was about 16 and on a visit to London, she decided to walk in Greenwich Park. It was autumn, and the leaves were turning colour and falling underfoot. Jane walked happily, accompanied by a servant, when quite suddenly she was seized from behind by a ruffian named Joseph Walsh, who without further ado bundled her into a waiting coach and made off as fast as possible. A boat was waiting for them and Jane, sick with terror, was bundled unceremoniously aboard and taken to Dunkirk, the then favourite haunt of many who skated only just this side of the law. Here, Joseph Walsh 'married' her.

Lady Puckering was in a terrible state, and it was decreed that steps should be taken for the recovery of poor Jane. The Council of State ordered all the necessary arrangements to be made, once they received the necessary petition setting forth details of the 'foul act at Greenwich'. A pass was given to a Mrs Magdalen Smith to go to Dunkirk and find out all she could. She was to take letters to parliamentary agents there and enlist their aid, and meanwhile a Mr Frost was to confer with ambassadors.

By early November things were moving, and a Colonel Popham was ordered to take a suitable ship to Nieuport, Flanders, and wait there to receive Jane on board. It seems Mrs Smith and Mr Frost had been successful in their negotiations. Jane was to have the best accommodation and the best care the ship could offer. Meanwhile poor Lady Puckering was offering up prayers for her daughter's safe deliverance and wringing her hands at Warwick Priory.

Poor Jane did get back! How much she suffered physically or mentally from this traumatic experience, we know not. The legal eagles got busy and the ridiculous 'marriage' to the ruffian Joseph Walsh was declared null and void.

Jane settled down for an all too brief while with her mother at Warwick Priory. Then, seeking to do her duty by her daughter, the Lady arranged her marriage to Sir John Bate, and he and Jane were married in the summer of 1650.

It would be nice to say 'they all lived happily ever after' but it was not to be. Jane's ill health eventually got the better of her and, never strong, she died in childbirth on 27th January 1652.

Thus ended the heiress of the Puckerings, and indeed the Puckerings themselves. Sir Henry Newton, a nephew of Sir Thomas, inherited upon Jane's death, and he assumed the name Puckering. He died in 1701, and the old Priory passed from one hand to another, until it eventually began to fall into disrepair.

In 1925, an American, Mr Alexander Wilbourne Weddell, bought Warwick Priory when it was put up for auction, and had it dismantled. It was then shipped over to Richmond, Virginia, and there re-erected, stone by stone, the main feature being its wonderfully-carved 17th-century staircase, down which the tragic heiress, little Miss Jane Puckering, may well have lightly tripped.

The Gunpowder Plotters

'GUNPOWDER, treason and plot. . . .' says the old rhyme, and the 'treason and plot' in this particular instance was first conceived in Warwickshire, by an ill-assorted group of men who were seeking to change the order of things, and bring off a coup! At least, that is what it would be called in today's jargon.

Robert Catesby was the prime mover in all this. He was born at Bushwood Hall, Lapworth in Warwickshire in 1573, and was a direct descendant of William Catesby, the loyal and faithful minister to Richard III who lost his life shortly after his royal master lost the battle of Bosworth.

The Catesbys were ardent Catholic converts, and Robert Catesby was a man of forceful character; good looking, a good organiser, a born 'leader'. As he saw about him adherents of the Old Faith, his faith, suffering the loss of liberty, wealth and position, the idea was gradually borne in upon him that these were 'his people' and it was up to him to lead them, to right their wrongs, and put an end to religious persecution.

He began to gather around him carefully selected conspirators. There was Tom Winter, an impoverished Worcestershire squire; Jack Wright and his brother Kit, minor gentry from a northern county; and there was an experienced sapper, born in York, who had gained much knowledge from service in the Low Countries, by the name of Guy Fawkes.

The plan was straightforward enough. To cause an explosion that would kill King James, Prince Henry and all the nobles assembled for the opening of Parliament on 5th November 1605. They were then to seize Prince Charles, or in default of him, the Princess Elizabeth, who was staying with Lord Harrington at the recently-built Coombe Abbey, just outside Coventry.

The conspirators would then rule the country, with one or other of the Royal children as puppet monarch, for whom a suitable marriage would rapidly be arranged with a loyal Catholic prince or princess.

It was an essential part of the plan to occupy one of the small houses adjacent to the Houses of Parliament, and a small tenement in Parliament Place was selected. Its lease presented some difficulties, since it was in the hands of the noted Warwickshire antiquary, Henry Ferrers of Baddesley Clinton, a neighbour of Catesby's at Lapworth, and one who knew him well for a Catholic rebel. Ferrers would wonder why Catesby wanted the lease, would suspect something, and refuse him. Therefore Thomas Percy, a kinsman of the Duke of Northumberland, who had fairly recently married Jack Wright's sister, was made privy to the plot and obtained the lease from Ferrers on some trumped-up story.

Under the command of Guy Fawkes, they began to store their gunpowder in the house. While this was being done, the rest of the conspirators were instructed to raise both money and horses. The money was to buy guns and ammunition to be used in the capture of the Princess Elizabeth at Coombe Abbey.

John Grant, the husband of Tom Winter's sister, had a large house at Norbrook, between Sherborne and Warwick. This was considered sufficiently isolated to be an appropriate rendezvous and to store the guns and ammunition. The ample stables were quite suddenly filled to overflowing as horses were acquired and sent there to provide transport for all the men involved in the plot.

The number of plotters grew, as it became necessary to take care of all contingencies and to spread the net. Sir Everard Digby took up temporary residence at Coughton Court, near Alcester, Warwickshire, the home before her marriage of Catesby's mother. Ambrose Rokewood took Clopton House, Stratford-on-Avon, on lease, and moved himself in there.

Everybody knew just what they had to do, and it was arranged that all of them would meet at the Lion Inn, Dunchurch, quite close to Rugby. They would seem to be a hunting party, and as soon a messenger rode in from London with the news of the success of their plan, they would all ride off to Coombe Abbey and capture the Princess.

They waited impatiently on the 4th and 5th November, carefully playing their allotted role as a hunting party so as not to alert the locals and the landlord. But the news, when it did arrive, was that their plan had miscarried. Fawkes was captured and in gaol. They had better fly for their lives!

Winter rode straightway to Coughton Court to warn the conspirators there to get themselves off somewhere to safety. The rest of the party rode frantically through Princethorpe, Weston and Lillington, thence to Warwick Castle and on to Norbrook, where they changed horses, and instantly rode off again.

The main party of conspirators were eventually run to ground at Holbeche, the home of Stephen Littleton, with the Sheriff of Worcester and his men hot on their heels. Tom Winter was shot in his right arm, Catesby and Percy were shot dead as they stood in the doorway, and the rest of them gave up and were taken prisoner.

The lesser members of the party fled through Warwickshire, and were eventually taken captive lurking in Snitterfield bushes.

On 23rd November, Winter confessed and the rest, realising all was lost, followed suit. They were all tried and hanged.

113

How the plot was discovered remains something of a mystery, but it is believed that it was one of the conspirators who got 'cold feet' and sent an anonymous letter to Lord Monteagle:

> 'My lord, out of the love i beare to some of your friends i have a caer of your preservacion therefore i would advyse youe as youe tender your lyf to devyse some excuse to shift youer attendance at this parlement. . . .'

Suspicion fell upon Tresham of Rushdon, Northants, as the writer of this letter, but it is extremely likely that something was already known of the plot before it was actually received.

Certainly Lord Harrington had already learned something of what was afoot, for even as the plotters waited at Dunchurch, he had ridden frantically to Coombe Abbey, and with armed men had taken away the young Princess Elizabeth. They rode with her to Coventry, and there they hid her in Palace Yard with the loyal citizens of Coventry promising to guard her with their lives.

Thus with the execution of a group of misguided martyrs ended the hopes of the Catholics in England that this country might eventually return to the Old Faith.

The Wicked Lady Dorothy

'FOR want of a shoe the horse was lost. . . .' Thus goes the old proverb, only in this particular instance, for want of a shoe not only was the horse lost, but so was Lady Dorothy Smyth.

The story begins in Wolvey, a small village on the northeast side of the county, where two ancient roads, Watling Street and the Fosseway, meet. About a mile north of Wolvey lies Shelford, formerly known as Shireford, and here was once set the lovely old manor house belonging to Henry Smyth, a wealthy mercer of Spon Street, Coventry. Henry Smyth had worked hard and prospered, and when he died in the 16th century, his son Walter was able to inherit quite a large estate.

Sir Walter Smyth married, and had but one son, Richard. The young man was grown up when his mother died, and Sir Walter was himself getting elderly. He decided it was time Richard was married, and he set about looking for a suitable wife. He wanted a good marriage for his son, and was determined to have it.

He talked the matter over with an acquaintance, Thomas Chetwin, a man of a good old family and a fine estate over the borders in Staffordshire, and Thomas Chetwin suggested his youngest daughter, Dorothy, who had a dowry of £500, might well fit the bill.

Sir Walter met the young Dorothy, and was instantly captivated by her beauty. There was no way in which Sir Walter would consider her for his son, but he must needs have her himself. He was besotted, and declared to her father that he would give him the £500 that he might have the lady for his wife.

Mr Chetwin, with his eye on the main chance, accepted, and persuaded his daughter that she must accept Sir William as her husband. In vain did she plead that she was young, and Sir William was old. She was told to do as she was told, and her future was assured. She really didn't have much choice.

The Lady Dorothy was forthwith married to the ageing Sir Walter, and went to live in the old manor house at Shireford, together with Richard Smyth, who obviously resented the arrangement.

It was not long before there was trouble. Sir Walter remained totally enamoured of his young wife, but she didn't take more than a week or two to get fed up with him.

She began an affair with a young man of her own age, Mr William Robinson of Drayton Bassett, who had the great fortune to be not only good looking, but rich as well. They were secret and they were discreet, and it is highly probable that Mr Robinson not only enjoyed his affair with the lady, but rather relished the intrigue as well.

However, Lady Dorothy determined to be rid of her husband, so that she might marry Mr Robinson. Sir Walter seemed to be in good health for his age and showed absolutely no predisposition to give up the ghost in order to please her. So she decided to take matters into her own hands.

She took into her confidence her waiting woman and a groom, and promised them money if they would help her. Mr Robinson was also supposed to be in on the act, but good sense prevailed and at the last minute he cried off.

That night the Lady Dorothy lay beside her husband until she was certain he was sound asleep, and then at a given signal the waiting woman and the groom came into the bedchamber to help her murder him. She put a long towel around his neck and twisted it, she pulling at the one end, and the waiting woman on the other. Sir Walter tried to put up a fight, and at one stage called out to her, 'Help me, Doll. . . .', before he realised that it was she who was seeking to stop his breath. Ultimately, the groom had to cast himself upon Sir Walter to stifle his struggles, until at last his breath stopped and he was dead.

They then manhandled the poor old man into the next chamber and sat him upon a close-stool. Evidence of the crime removed, the waiting woman and the groom returned to their quarters.

In the morning Lady Dorothy 'awoke' with a loud cry, insisting that the servants make an immediate search for her husband who had stolen from her side in the night. As she had planned, the servants found him upon the close-stool in the next room, dead.

Lady Dorothy's public lamentations were quite fearful, but she made a rapid recovery and soon after Sir Walter's remains were decently disposed of, she went to London where, as a beautiful and wealthy widow, she was much fêted. She had grown both proud and vain by this time, and Mr Robinson, although he looked her up in town, was roundly snubbed for not playing his rightful part in her widowhood.

More than a year later, Richard Smyth had to go into Coventry upon a business matter, and chanced to take with him the groom who had been of such assistance to the Lady Dorothy. They had a jolly time, visited a few alehouses, and the groom in his cups was smitten by drunkard's remorse and told Richard Smyth everything.

When he woke up the following morning with a hangover, he realised what he had done, and stole his master's horse and make good his escape. But Richard acted quickly and had him safely brought back. He also laid information against Lady Dorothy and the waiting woman, and they too were brought prisoners to Warwick.

Lady Dorothy denied everything, and accused Richard of making the whole thing up in order to get his father's money the sooner. The groom, realising all was lost, stuck to his story, and eventually the waiting woman too gave way and told the truth.

The groom and waiting woman were sentenced to be hanged at Warwick, but there was a definite suspicion of witchcraft about Lady Dorothy. It was suggested that witchcraft must have been used to snare a wily old bird like Sir Walter into marriage, and that she had used withcraft to force the servants to help her despatch him.

Hanging was, therefore, too good for Lady Dorothy. She was to be burnt at the stake.

In the year 1555, two years exactly after the murder of her husband, the Lady Dorothy was publicly bound to a stake set atop a pile of faggots, on the wild sparse hermitage land at Wolvey Heath. She was still very young, and very beautiful, but the mere mention of witchcraft struck terror into the hearts of the populace, and there was no one to save her. The torch was applied to the faggots, and in a very short time the figure of Lady Dorothy could no more be seen through the flames.

All was over when the horse and rider, lathered with sweat, arrived bearing a reprieve for the Lady. Alas, the horse had cast a shoe and . . . all was lost.

The Martyrs of Mancetter

MANCETTER is in north Warwickshire, and despite the fairly close proximity of mining activities, Mancetter is a pretty village, still rural in character, still green and tree-lined.

The manor house stands close by the church. Believed to be 14th century in origin, it has been added to by its various owners over the centuries, and presents a fine black-and-white timbered face to the world.

It was once the home of the Glover family, who worshipped in the little church on their doorstep. A good family, their three sons had but recently returned from Cambridge, where they had learned to question religious beliefs. They were not 'rabble rousers' nor hot-heads, but just wanted to live the quiet life of a country squire, and to worship as they pleased.

But this they were not allowed to do, once 'Bloody Mary' ascended the throne of England in 1553. In no time at all, Queen Mary had set the country ablaze in more ways than one.

One of the first to be dealt with was Bishop Hugh Latimer. He had taken the King's (Henry VIII) side when he wanted to dissolve his marriage with Catherine of Aragon, Mary's mother. This naturally meant that Mary was ill-disposed towards him, and he was a marked man. The gentle Latimer went to the stake for heresy in Oxford, on a site opposite Balliol College.

Hugh Latimer was known in Mancetter. Robert Glover was married to his niece, and Latimer had often visited them at the manor house. He once preached in the church, attended by Augustine Bernher, the saintly cleric of Southam.

Queen Mary was a zealot, and was determined to rid the country of heresy. She appointed Dr Ralph Banes as Bishop of Lichfield and Coventry and he, with an eye to his future career, was equally assiduous in the rounding up of heretics.

The Glovers had made no secret of their religious beliefs; they were Protestants. Hearing of this, and hearing that Mistress Glover was the niece of Hugh Latimer, Banes ordered the arrest of the Glover brothers.

The Sheriff's men were to ride out, and bring them back to gaol. But the Mayor of Coventry knew the Glovers, and liked them. They had done business together, and he knew them for honourable men, not ranting heretics. Out of the kindness of his heart, he sent a servant on ahead of the Sheriff's men to warn them.

The servant arrived in time, and John and William fled into the forest which in those days surrounded Mancetter; but Robert could not move. He was lying ill in bed in his chamber, shivering with the fever, and could not stir. In any case, when the Sheriff's men arrived, it was found that by some error his name was not on the warrant, only that of John and William.

The Sheriff was all for leaving Robert alone, and riding back to Coventry, but his men were not so easily dissuaded. For one thing, they were frightened of the wrath of Dr Banes, and it was fear for their own skins that made them gather up the sick Robert Glover and carry him back to Coventry.

Banes questioned him hour upon hour, about the true nature of the sacraments, the mass, the confession of sins and so forth, and found Robert Glover's replies totally unacceptable.

Robert Glover was sentenced to be burnt at the stake, and was flung back into the prison to await his death. While there, he received frequent visits from the kindly little Augustine Bernher, who risked his own life to bring him comfort. There are many who have referred to Bernher as the 'Uncanonised Saint'.

On 20th September, 1555, Robert Glover met his fearful death. His last act on earth was to write a letter to his wife at Mancetter.

Glover faltered slightly in his faith towards the end, and Bernher later wrote an account of this. However, it seems that as Glover walked slowly towards the stake, the chains and the pile of faggots that awaited him, he suddenly appeared to see a divine vision. His face shone, and a smile wreathed his lips. Clasping his hands together, he cried 'He is come' and he then stepped joyfully, even jauntily, up to his funeral pyre.

His brothers John and William did not long survive him. John remained hidden in the woods, and narrowly escaped capture on two occasions. He had been declared excommunicate. Then cold, exposure and malnutrition caught up with him, and these he could not escape. He died their captive.

He was very quietly and secretly buried in Mancetter churchyard, but not apparently secretly enough, even though no Church service was read over his pitiful remains. It came to the notice of the Chancellor of the Diocese, who doubtless wished to curry favour with Bishop Banes, and he ordered that the remains of the body of John Glover should be taken from the grave by the vicar, and cast over the churchyard wall into the public highway, that people might walk upon them. In vain did the vicar protest that the man had been buried more than two months. He was told to obey orders, and when the body of the heretic had left the grave, the ground around it must needs be reconsecrated.

William Glover fled to Shropshire, where he too subsequently died within a couple of years. But the arm of the Church is a long one. The curate at Wem, Shropshire, refused to bury poor William's corpse unless given leave to do so. While he waited for his instructions, a kindly villager attempted to remove William from the church porch, but was prevented by those afraid of the authority of the Church.

Banes' instructions came at last. William was excommunicated, and could not therefore be buried in consecrated ground. His body was taken away in a dung cart, and put in a hole in a field near the parish boundary.

The courage of the Glovers had left an impression, though, notably upon their neighbour at Mancetter. Mrs Joyce Lewis and her husband Thomas lived quite close to the manor house, and although they had hitherto been staunch Roman Catholics, the steadfastness of the Glovers, and the fearful treatment they received at the hands of the Church, impressed Joyce very much. So much, in fact, that she refused to accompany her husband to church on Sundays, and received a strong warning from the vicar.

Her husband Thomas reasoned with her, and begged her to reconsider, but Joyce declared she could no longer attend Mass.

Eventually the much-feared summons came from Bishop Banes. Joyce Lewis was arrested and flung into gaol to await questioning. Banes questioned, Joyce answered, and again the answers branded her a heretic. She was sentenced to the stake.

Joyce Lewis, however, was quite undaunted. Even when chained to the stake with the flames licking her feet, Joyce Lewis continued to smile serenely, to the astonishment of the crowd gathered round about her.

Robert Glover and Joyce Lewis, the Mancetter Martyrs, are commemorated in the little church at Mancetter. The pinnacled tower at nearby Baxterley church was raised by Hugh Glover, son of Robert, in memory of his brave father.

The Ploughboy MP

THE agricultural labourer of the 19th century suffered acute and dire poverty; living in tiny, cramped and damp tied cottages, and working long hours for a desperately poor wage. However, a Warwickshire man from the village of Barford, rose among their ranks to be their champion and he fought his way from the ditches of his native heath to the benches of Westminster to plead their cause.

Barford lies along the curve of the Avon, about three miles from the county town of Warwick, and in a tiny cottage in Church Street, Joseph Arch was born in November 1826, the youngest child of John and Hannah Arch.

Hannah's parents, John and Mary Pace, had been servants at Warwick Castle, living in one of the castle lodges. Thriftily they had saved all the coppers tossed to them by visiting gentry for whom they opened the lodge gates, and managed to save the sum of £35 with which they bought their own cottage at Barford.

Hannah too was a castle servant, and married one of the coachmen, but when he died, Hannah married John Arch. Hannah and John moved into the cottage at Barford upon the death of John Pace, and looked after Hannah's widowed mother. It was here that two girls, Mary and Ann, and two boys, John and Joseph, were born to them. John died in infancy, and Joseph became the 'baby' of the family and the apple of his mother's eye.

Hannah was a strong-willed and determined woman. A fighter, filled with an independent spirit, which she seems to have passed on in full measure to her youngest child. Joseph attended the village school, and was encouraged both by his schoolmaster and his mother in self-help and self-education.

The Arch family were slightly better off than most agricultural labouring families in that they owned their cottage, and were not therefore dependent upon the foibles of farmer-owners. They needed to find no rent, and their garden provided most of the family's food. In Joseph's own words, 'It was choke-full of vegetables and fruit in season. . . .' Charity bread and soup were dispensed to the poor of Barford, but Joseph never had any. Hannah's independent spirit would have none of it, and Joseph recalled how she was saddened by the sight of labourers' children, with their toes out of their boots, going past carrying tin cans for their soup.

Joseph was forced to leave school at the age of nine, and seek work. His first job was crow-scaring at the rate of 4d for a twelve-hour day, but at the age of twelve he obtained work as a ploughboy at the rate of 3s a week.

He later described how he crept to work, half asleep, in the dark in the early hours of the morning, with a hunk of barley bread, or an apple baked in a paste of coarse wheatmeal, wrapped in a cloth for his day's food.

Joseph Arch persevered with his education. He read whatever came his way, he joined the village friendly society; he spent any few coppers he had to spare on secondhand newspapers and became immersed in the speeches of Gladstone and John Bright, men whom he greatly admired.

Hannah had always believed the Church extended too much influence of the wrong kind on the lives of poor people, so when some Methodist preachers, 'rough and ready men from Wellesbourne', began holding meetings in a barn in Barford, Hannah and Joseph attended. Joseph later became a Primitive Methodist lay preacher.

In 1847, Hannah Arch died, and this was a great blow to Joseph. She had been the mainspring of the entire family, holding it together, guiding him, managing his father, and making their small income buy all they needed. 'It was an empty time', Joseph said later.

Shortly after this, Joseph Arch married Mary Ann Mills, a domestic servant from Wellesbourne, and she moved into the cottage at Barford to look after Joseph and his father. With a wife, and a family to look after, Joseph Arch was now poorer than he had ever been before.

With his interest in politics, Joseph had long felt the agricultural labourer to be very unjustly treated. He had made himself into what he called 'a good all-rounder', for not only could he plough, but he was a first-class hedger and ditcher, could turn his hand to carpentry, make coffins and hang a gate. In fact, he won prizes for his skills at Wellesbourne Ploughing Society shows.

He decided to embark upon what we would now call 'contracting' and he hired himself out to any employer to do any specific job. He tramped all through the Midland counties, going from job to job, sleeping rough in barns, and working incredibly hard, but he earned more money that way.

But he went around with his eyes wide open, and what he saw saddened him. Poverty and misery were widespread, but at that time he had no idea what he could do about it.

There had already been several abortive attempts to start an agricultural union, but the labourers were frightened. At the very mention of the word, their employers would have had them out on their ear.

Then, on a dull and miserable wet day, 7th February 1872, Joseph Arch was visited at his home by two labourers from nearby Wellesbourne. They asked him to conduct a union meeting at Wellesbourne that evening. They said they needed a man of strength and determination, who could inspire confidence, and Joseph could certainly do that. Furthermore, because he was a 'freelance' and did not live in a tied cottage, he was unable to be put off or evicted as others might be.

Joseph agreed, and set off to walk to Wellesbourne that night, wearing his ordinary working clothes, and an old flannel jacket, which he later kept as a souvenir of this momentous occasion.

An enormous crowd had gathered on Wellesbourne village green. Some local dignitary had seen to it that the lamps around the village green were unlit, but that had not deterred the labourers, for they had lanterns to light the scene, and many of them had walked for miles to be present at this meeting. Mounted on a pig-killing stool, looking down upon faces gaunt with hunger and want, Joseph Arch felt 'the call' had come to him to help his fellow men.

Many more meetings followed and Joseph Arch tramped the country, addressing thousands of poverty-stricken labourers, and urging them to form themselves into a union. Joseph Arch kindled a flame, and from this humble beginning the National Agricultural Labourers Union was formed.

The members of this union suffered even greater hardship and want than usual when they lost their employment, and their families were often turned out of their tied cottages, but nothing could stop them now. They had nothing to lose but misery.

Joseph later fought for the extension of the franchise to give the labourer the vote, and this was finally achieved in 1884. The following year, Joseph Arch became a parliamentary candidate, and was elected Liberal MP for the constituency of North West Norfolk.

Joseph Arch, the champion ploughboy, had come a long way. But he did not forget his roots, for he eventually came back to live at Barford, and he died there in the cottage where he was born.

The famous 'Wellesbourne tree' died in 1948, but the spot is marked by a commemorative stone, and a replacement tree was planted in 1949. A plaque set at its foot records the story of Joseph Arch's 'glorious work'.